Come to me ...

A resource for weary Christians and those who care about them

Raymond Tomkinson

Raymond Tomkinson

5.2.01

First published in 2000 by
KEVIN MAYHEW LTD
Buxhall
Stowmarket
Suffolk IP14 3BW

The publishers wish to express their gratitude to:

North American Liturgy Resources (NALR), 5536 NE Hassalo,
Portland, OR 97213, USA for permission to use the extract from
We behold the splendour (Transfiguration) by Carey Landry.
All rights reserved.

Scripture quotations are taken from:

New Revised Standard Version of the Bible, copyright 1989 by the
Division of Christian Education of the National Council of the
Churches of Christ in the USA.

Revised English Bible, © Oxford University and
Cambridge University Presses, 1989.

Used by permission. All rights reserved

0 1 2 3 4 5 6 7 8 9

ISBN 1 84003 552 8
Catalogue No. 1500354

Cover design by Jonathan Stroulger
Typesetting by Richard Weaver
Printed in Great Britain

This book is dedicated to my dear wife Rose in the twenty-fifth year of our marriage.

Acknowledgements

Although this project has been pleasurable, the subject has caused me to revisit my own feelings, and to explore in some depth my own relationship with God and his Church. This has from time to time made me reflective, quiet and pensive. Many thanks therefore to my beloved wife Rose, and daughter Marian, for their understanding and encouragement. They have seen me through the project with characteristic compassion, common sense, and love. Their observations, insights and comments have been immensely valuable.

I am deeply indebted to The Revd Professor Mark Williams, Director of the Institute of Medical and Social Care Research, and Pro Vice-Chancellor of the University of Wales, Bangor, who has encouraged me throughout this project. Without his professional advice, profound wisdom and personal friendship I would not have been able to complete this work.

So many people have been supportive that it is hazardous to mention only a few but I would like to thank Philip Collins for his endless patience, for his prayerful support and spiritual advice. Thanks also to so many good friends and colleagues for their loyalty and encouragement. Last, but by no means least, I would like to thank the people whose own experiences of weariness, shared in confidence, have contributed to this book.

Contents

*Come to me, all who are weary
and whose load is heavy;
I will give you rest.*

Matthew 11:28
Revised English Bible

Foreword

It is sometimes very subtle, but it happens more often than we care to think: judging ourselves and others by how much activity we can see. Part of the problem is that we see tiredness and weariness as the enemy. We do battle with it, increasing our sense of exhaustion. In this book, Raymond Tomkinson offers us an alternative view. Little by little, through extended metaphor, story and biblical reflection, he builds for us a coherent theology of weariness. He writes of how God can use exhaustion for his own purpose, and of how tiredness has meaning in and of itself. Drawing from his experience as a professional nurse, as a parish priest in the Church of England, and as a spiritual director, Raymond Tomkinson's exploration shows us how our weariness can reveal to us aspects of our relationship with God we had never before been aware of.

From his own experience of Chronic Fatigue Syndrome, discussed frankly and openly in the book, he shows how weariness, and the rest that it demands, can be blessed by God in its own right. For example, the exhaustion that makes a person hypersensitive to loud noise or bright light can bring with it an increased sensitivity to the presence of God. Such a state of mind can bring with it also a new way of honouring our bodies, of valuing economy of effort. It can show us the possibility of a twenty-four-hour relationship with God, and how to use sleep as prayer.

So the book provides a way of acknowledging weariness for what it is; not the enemy, but a potential guide to greater depths of being. And because weariness is so 'infectious', the book is also written for those who care for others for whom exhaustion is never far away. Raymond Tomkinson's book allows us to see how this state need not be seen as a weakness, but rather as an opportunity to deepen faith. His argument is sound, both psychologically and theologically. I warmly commend the book to you.

Revd Professor Mark Williams, DSc, FBPsS,
Director, Institute of Medical and Social Care Research
and Pro Vice-Chancellor, University of Wales, Bangor.

Introduction

There are a whole range of people, including Christians, who see life from within an experience of weakness, frailty, weariness or vulnerability and who are sensitive to the constructs of others as presented to them in preaching, teaching, attitudes and prejudice.

The Scriptures and the writings of Christian authors have been a great source of encouragement and enlightenment. However, from within the hypersensitivity brought on by an experience of weakness, fatigue and frailty, some of those Scriptures and writings can have an adverse effect.

I have made several references to suffering from what we now call Chronic Fatigue Syndrome, formerly called Myalgic Encephalomyelitis (M.E.). I contracted this illness in the spring of 1988. My perspective is coloured by this experience as I have sought to make sense of it and to reflect theologically upon it. In my search for meaning I turned to the Scriptures and discovered (or rediscovered) helpful passages. I have been challenged by other passages that seem to disenfranchise me: so many Scriptures that speak of strength, vitality and activity in the service of the Lord, making much of the ability to fight; to run the race; to overcome; to strive. Inability to do any or all of these things, all of the time, is regarded negatively and defined as failure, weakness, sloth, or moral weakness. This may engender guilt, hopelessness and despair, further disabling and making more difficult the striving, running, fighting and the like.

It may appear that the traditional 'authorities' are being denigrated. The aim is to start from the position of those oppressed by the 'wisdom' and to work through the conflict to a point where hope and confidence can be renewed: including hope and confidence in those same authorities.

Through this book I hope to promote those Scriptures which

indicate how God works in weakness, passivity and receptivity, and not in spite of it. In writing something of a polemic against the culture, I want to offer a way in which we can be compassionate towards ourselves and towards each other. I want to explore with the reader a view of God (in Scripture and tradition) which speaks of warm and constant love, and a cautionary word to a Church with a mixed message to its ministers and others.

My perspective has also been influenced by my experience of the Church and how it uses the Scriptures to promote the strong and active, disabling people like me. I began to think that the Church had either become a victim of a late twentieth-century 'workaholic' culture or worse: the Church had promoted the culture more than two hundred years ago by the development of the Protestant work ethic. In contradiction, I have heard preachers and pastors speak out against that very culture, encouraging people to take a retreat, to rest, to be still. As a nurse and a pastor I have met people who, like me, have looked for God in their weariness and have been discouraged by certain of the Scriptures and by those who expound them.

Writing for the weary, I make no attempt to identify the cause of weariness because I am not qualified to do so. Those who are weary know who they are. They may know that their condition is temporary. They may know they have been working too hard. They may be mentally or physically ill. Their illness may be acute or chronic. They may not know why they are weary. They may be too weary to find out. Whoever they are, they may have been searching for understanding, acceptance, encouragement and meaning. Their weariness may be compounded by despondency or guilt.

The first two chapters challenge popular definitions of strength, weakness and brokenness and offer alternative and more encouraging views, whilst Chapter 3 offers some reflection on western culture of the late twentieth century, which is characterised by frenzied activity, unreasonable expectations, and competitiveness fuelled by the Protestant work ethic. The reader is encouraged to explore the scriptural use of 'night' in both its literal and metaphorical senses. Ways of understanding prayer and praying amidst an experience of weariness are explored in Chapter 4.

Chapters 5 and 6 afford an opportunity to examine other factors that impact upon weary people and explore strategies for coping better. There is reflection on what motivates and de-motivates people, and, using the story of David and Goliath, the reader is encouraged to find ways to make the most of their limited physical, mental, emotional, and spiritual resources. Finally, in Chapter 7, the themes of the book are drawn together around two poignant and intimate accounts in the Gospels.

To some extent each chapter stands alone, allowing the read-ers to read where they feel drawn. From experience, those attracted by the sub-title 'A resource for weary Christians . . .' do not want a heavy tome that wakes one up as it hits the bed-room floor! This is a book which does not compel one to read on and avoids making one feel guilty if it is left unfinished. It may be useful to those spending some time 'apart' but it is also for those sharing with others in a safe environment, perhaps in a house group or discussion group. At the end of each chapter, in addition to references, there is a biblical text as a suggested focus for reflection. There are also some suggestions for prayer, questions for those alone and some ideas to stimulate group discussion.

Raymond D. Tomkinson, September 1999

Chapter 1

Definitions of 'strength' and 'weakness': how they feed our guilt

Many are wearied from the battle against physical, mental, emotional or spiritual ill health. They may be battling with a potent combination of these and the more they battle, the more they are weakened. The word 'weak' or 'weakness' taunts the weary for it brings with it a connotation of blame. There is the unspoken insinuation (real or imagined) that one would not be weak if only one had the will to be strong.

We live in a 'mind over matter' culture. It seems that anything can be conquered if only we have the will-power. To be strong is good and heroic; to be weak is contemptuous. We may work with those weakened and wearied by grief, depression or redundancy, and we can pour out compassion and understanding. We can be enraged by the way society marginalises them and disempowers them. But, just occasionally, after another long session, even the most patient and the most generous of us can entertain a pejorative thought: 'If this person had the will, they could be stronger.' At that point we join the ranks of those who hold that only the fittest deserve to survive. No matter how hard we try to ignore it, a tiny voice tells us that weakness is something that can be overcome if there is a will to overcome it.

When I first succumbed to Chronic Fatigue Syndrome[1] I became too weak to walk very far unaided. A flight of stairs might as well have been Mount Everest. To comb what little hair I have was exhausting. Lifting the comb to my scalp caused muscle fatigue and pain more akin to having done one hundred press-ups when out of condition.

Previously I had enough strength to hold down a full-time and demanding job; to be busy with many hobbies and the demands of a home and family. Now I was weak and dependent upon others for some of the most fundamental human needs. Many were sympathetic but some, I know, were of the mind, at least some of the time, that I could overcome my weakness by will-power alone.

It can become easy for someone who is suffering from physical weakness to believe that they are morally weak. They begin to ask themselves if it could be true that they cannot overcome their weakness (or weariness) because they lack moral fibre. This kind of subjective thinking is often part of the picture. It simply compounds feelings of guilt and lowers morale. The consequence can be that it is harder than ever to summon emotional or spiritual resources to aid recovery.

Certainly it is important to have a positive attitude of mind. I needed regular encouragement and counsel to set targets for myself so that I felt I was making progress. Many times the targets were unrealistic and I had to start again. Sometimes the targets were so unrealistic that I caused myself more harm than good and set back my recovery.

Occasionally, I would have bursts of irrational energy and set about tasks in a frenzied way only to collapse with exhaustion. Then it would take weeks to regain lost ground. Sometimes, out of anger, frustration or pride, I would do far too much and pay the price in regression and defeat.

I knew both strength and weakness in my wearied state, but, in the early years, the times of capitulation and exhaustion were in the majority. It was then that I had time to consider the meaning of strength and weakness. Some years on, my weariness has been accommodated and my resources are carefully managed. Now I am neither strong nor weak but, when I need to, I can take considered risks and can summon the energy required.

I have not, however, come to terms with weakness as being something I cannot help. Perhaps resisting that notion keeps me trying to overcome obstacles, though not to the point of counter-productive effort. I remain haunted by a popular definition of 'weak' and 'weakness' that is judgemental. There remain times, though less often now, when I imagine that my weakness is perceived as moral weakness. I still meet people who clearly regard my condition as being 'all in the mind' – which, to them, equates with moral weakness.

I strongly defend the view that, even if it were true that my condition is entirely mental, it has nothing to do with my moral strength.

Perhaps it helps to approach the issue of weakness from another perspective: I have a weakness for meringues. If having a weakness for meringues is a crime, then I stand guilty. If I were to come before a judge I would ask for a number of other crimes to be taken into consideration. These would include a weakness for Turkish Delight, sugared almonds and chocolate eclairs: 'Yes, I admit it, M'lord, I have a sweet tooth, I cannot help it.'

I feel guilty about my weakness perhaps because I have heard that these things are not good for me. In this sense, weakness is defined for me as a tendency to eat (and to enjoy) that which is not thought to be good for me. Nowadays I avoid added sugar and indulge only occasionally in my favourite desserts. My sweet tooth has not been surgically removed nor have I been through therapy. I know I am only one cake shop away from disaster. I have the ability to resist sweet things (I probably always had) but I do so now because I know they do not give me the boost of energy I need without making me put on weight, which won't help me in the long term.

By the same token, nutritionists would caution me about the need for fibre; the need to avoid saturated fats; and the dangers of alcohol and stimulating drinks. Vegetarians counsel me about the evils of eating meat. Organic farmers worry me about pesticides on my fruit and vegetables. If I thought about it too much I would eat nothing: certainly nothing I really enjoy, but should I feel guilty for succumbing to what others regard as weakness of the human condition?

Sadly, guilt is part of the process: part of the experience. It will include the way we have indulged our so-called weaknesses to the detriment of our health. My point is that weakness is defined for us by others. Weakness is our failure to comply with the teaching or philosophy of others or to conform to their stereotype of strength.

The weary include those who are flattened, worn out, by the bombardment of advice and counsel, propaganda, emotional blackmail, cajolement, sarcasm and criticism of others. Judgement is being passed upon us about our perceived weakness in relation to another's perception of strength and the ability to resist. This makes weakness a subjective judgement.

It seems that weakness is nearly always regarded as something negative: something to be avoided. Being strong, resisting temptation, suffering and striving to overcome weakness – these are virtues to be admired. We hear of those who have overcome great difficulties; those who have suffered from great calamities, who have clawed their way out of whatever pit they found themselves in to stand erect, heads held high. The heroic achievements of others can have a demoralising effect. One can be left with the feeling that they must have some capacity that we have not. Weakness is equated with failure and failure breeds guilt. Unresolved guilt is debilitating and makes the sense of weakness worse.

The burden of external pressure to overcome weakness may not be the only thing that is making us weary. We can feel guilty that we cannot resist temptation or that we cannot give up a habit, an attitude, a relationship. We feel guilty that we have even entertained a negative thought about how we feel unable to overcome our weaknesses. We add to the burden of external pressure the burden of guilt and we stagger beneath the load. We become further demoralised and our weakness compounded. The chances of us overcoming the (so-called) weakness are further reduced because such energy as we might have been able to summon up has been used up in coping with the bombardment and the guilt.

Even if we find ourselves strong and able to make some progress in overcoming our difficulty we are not allowed to indulge ourselves in a little self-praise. The Christian ethos teaches us that all we are, and all we are able to do, is in God's strength and not in our own. We might have cried out in frustration that God did not seem to be there when our fingertips scratched at the walls of the abyss. As one priest friend of mine put it: 'It (prayer) is like screaming into a concrete bucket: you don't even get the echo back.' And yet, when the little resurrection comes out of the little death, it seems we must give God all the glory.

Could we not be encouraged to hold a view that God is the author of strength and life *and* of weakness and death? Hold the view, and leave it at that? Then, as we struggle and overcome, struggle and fail, we can be set free to take the broader view; the long-term view: the eternal view. Is not that preferable to becoming preoccupied with who did what in us and when? In that way God still gets the glory but our human efforts and minor achievements can be recognised. In the recognition of them we can allow ourselves some encouragement: some positive reinforcement that will keep us going through the next phase of our survival or recovery.

The underlying fear is that we will lose sight of God's grace: his transfiguring, transforming and healing grace. The worry is that we will attribute all our successes to ourselves. Possibly. It is more likely that without some human consolation or belief in our own capability we will remain so far down the abyss that we do not, in any case, recognise the God who shares the darkness with us. Sheila Cassidy has put this so well in her book, *Sharing the darkness*.[2] Through personal and professional experience Dr Cassidy is able to identify with those struggling in the darkness, trying to make sense of their situation. Her approach fuses the carer with the cared for in a mutuality of enlightenment, confusion, tears and joy. It is a far cry from the model of strong carer rescuing weak victim. It is also the theology of the crucified Saviour: of the withered hand that stretches out in healing.

When I was nursing, I cringed whenever I heard a well-meaning hospital chaplain attempting to remind a patient of the goodness of God. I cringed because of an incident early in my nursing career. The incident involved a patient (let's call him Bill), a man in his early seventies who was recovering from a stroke. Bill had faith in God. He had a nodding relationship with God. He enjoyed praise services on the television (provided that there were none of those modern choruses!). God was out there somewhere and he would admit to sending up the occasional prayer: 'God, help me through this.' He would make the odd bargain with God: 'Get my wife through this and I won't neglect her again.'

His stroke had left him paralysed down one side, his speech impaired, and his emotions labile. During the early days following the stroke, he was not expected to live. Lying in bed, purple and unconscious, his breathing heavy, his limbs flaccid, his family could only watch and hope and (perhaps) pray.

During the weeks that followed he had been pulled about and turned from side to side. Tubes had been inserted in most orifices. Strangers in starched linen had given him brief explanations, words of encouragement, instructions to be followed. He had lost more than physical motion and the power of speech. He had lost confidence, independence and hope. Tearfully he would grasp his wife's hand in his one good hand. In that grasp there was a cry for help and a need to believe that life could be the same as it was. Communicating his needs and desires was painfully slow and complicated. Picture cards helped a little, but focusing and concentrating was hard work. Constant care meant constant effort on his part as well as on the part of so many others. He had to learn how to use devices for pulling himself up the bed. He learned how to help those helping him in or out of bed. He had overcome incontinence through an exhausting programme called 'habit retraining'. Bathing was an ordeal in addition to the embarrassment of nakedness in front of strangers. All this he did.

With the help of a walking frame and flanked by a nurse and a physiotherapist, he took his first steps down the middle of the ward. Other patients called out: 'Come on, Bill, you can do it!' He smiled his lopsided smile and cried his lopsided tears and each step was taken with the effort of being born anew.

No sooner had Bill sunk, gratefully and heavily, into his chair when the hospital chaplain entered the ward. The other patients were still applauding and the chaplain asked why. Having been told of Bill's heroic efforts the chaplain exclaimed: 'Praise God, John! *(his name was Bill)* Look what he has done for you.' Bill smiled his lopsided smile and cried his lopsided tears.

Later, much later, he recalled his anger. Not that he doubted somewhere deep down that God had brought him through, but so had his own human efforts. He needed the encouragement of his achievement in making those first awkward steps. It was something he needed for himself: for his own sake. These were confidence-building moments that would lead him forward to the next little achievement and so on until he was able to live a reasonably independent life. 'No offence to the Padre,' he said, 'but his timing could not have been worse.'

In not allowing Bill to take some credit for his own achievement, the chaplain had managed to undermine the healing work of God. How sad it is that people are so keen to keep us humble that they incite in us anger and resentment and set back an understanding of God's strength in our weakness and our strength in his grace.

Months later, Bill returned to a fairly normal life. He would, once again, watch praise services on the television. He would send up the occasional prayer. His faith was none the worse for his encounter with the hospital chaplain. He knew in his heart that God had helped him through and he shared that inner knowledge with a sense of personal achievement.

No work on strength and weakness would be complete without reference to St Paul and his much-quoted: 'When I am weak, then I am strong'.[3] The inference is that God allowed Paul to keep his weaknesses because when he was weak, Christ within him could be more powerful. Weakness, leading to sin or self-harm, alienates us from Christ but some weakness is the inability to resist the power of Christ within us. Then, in our weakness, God is strong and so are we.

We begin to understand that there is no truly objective definition of weakness and we may have differentiated weakness that leads to sin and spiritual death from weakness that is the absence of strength to resist God. How often we concentrate on weakness that leads to sin and death – and how seldom we encourage the weakness that leads to grace and life!

Those who are weary are often accused of being slothful or indolent. Suggested remedies might include doing something active and energetic. The hope is that the right stimulus will help us to 'snap out' of our weary state. Comparatively few perceive that we can also be too weary to sin. Some sinning takes effort and energy. It takes the mental energy to organise and plan for an occasion of sin. Deception is an exhausting business: having to remember what one has said to whom. Having a weak memory may mean that one forgets to bear a grudge! Sometimes the weary cannot be bothered to sin. It is not the best of motives but it is better than none.

The more one ponders on the life of St Paul and the issues with which he wrestled, the more one suspects that he lost sight, at least sometimes, of the difference between strength and weakness. As Saul of Tarsus he once had attributes that might have been regarded as strengths: like being able to stand by and watch others stone young Stephen to death[4] – strengths he would later understand as sin.

We begin to see that weakness has both positive and negative attributes. Our choices might have been between being weak (over which we may feel we have no control) and being strong (which we may feel is unattainable). Now we see that our choice may be between weakness that is destructive, which may lead to sin and death; and weakness which allows the power of Christ capacity to transform us. Then, like Paul, we may come to the conclusion that our weakness has purpose: that it can be channelled, if not into strength then into constructive and appropriate weakness.

References

1. Chronic Fatigue Syndrome was formerly called Myalgic Encephalomyelitis (M.E.) A condition said to affect more than a hundred thousand people in the UK alone. The cause is unknown and the presentation varies, making diagnosis difficult. Characteristic symptoms include muscle aches and pains, continual fatigue even after rest, memory and concentration loss.
2. *Sharing the Darkness* by Dr Sheila Cassidy, Medical Director of St Luke's Hospice, Plymouth. Published by Darton, Longman & Todd.
3. 2 Corinthians 12:10.
4. Acts 7:54-end.

Focus for reflection

Who told you that you were naked? (Genesis 3:11)

Suggestions for prayer

Lord, how well everyone knows my weaknesses.
You know how fond I am of this and that:
    how I crave my fancies; indulge my passions;
    relish my favourite things.
Lord, you came that we might have life
    and have it in its fullness
    and yet there are those who preach to me
    about self-denial and abstinence.
Surely, when I am dead is time enough to abstain.
Economy, opportunity, fatigue
    prevent me from indulging myself too much;
    but keep me from gluttony,
    and the kind of self-indulgence which does you dishonour.
Teach me to savour what you provide
    in the way of treats and delights,
    fun and laughter.
Let me be human
    and help others to let me be fully alive. Amen.

Lord, help me to hear your voice
    among the many who bombard me
    with advice and counsel, propaganda, blackmail,
    cajoling, sarcasm and criticism.
Above it all I hear you say:
    'I love you with a perfect love.'
Lord, help me to discover your hand
    in choice and desire.
Teach me to lose that inherited voice
    that nags away at duty and denial,
    saying more to me of the problems of others
    than of your gentle alluring. Amen.

As I try, once again, to fight my weariness,
    teach me to let go:
    to risk that in sinking into fatigue,
    there is a net to catch me;
    a rest to heal me,
    and an oblivion from which to be reborn.
Catch hold of the guilt that weighs me down,
    that brings me crashing down to earth.
Lift it from me that I may soar
    high into the bliss of your presence:
    weightless, sinless, content.
So be it. Amen.

Lord, help the powerless.
Give voice to their plight.
Help us to be their voice, their champion,
    and their advocate,
    so that they may know the dignity of personhood,
    and themselves to be your children. Amen.

Questions for those alone

What do you regard as your weaknesses?

Who told you they were weaknesses, and what might have been their motives?

How might your weaknesses give God a chance to shape your life?

Suggestions for group discussion

Share definitions of weakness and strength and discuss how helpful or unhelpful they are.

How could someone's perceived weakness be interpreted as a strength?

Can we help others to celebrate weakness?

Chapter 2

Valuing brokenness:
celebrating what we shall become

I hate those great and sinister machines at garages and petrol stations that wash cars. As I sit in the car it appears to move forward on its own, out of my control. Great whirling brushes attack from both sides and move around me in a relentless and ominous way as they brush away dirt, grime, wing mirrors and aerials. I am at the mercy of the detergent-covered capsule and I pray that I will soon see clearly the green light that tells me to put the car in gear and to take off down the road. Those great brushes remind me of two enemies of the weary. Their names are Introspection and Unworthiness. They cause us to spend too much energy on self-analysis, self-deprecation and flagellation and yet, appropriately harnessed, they can help us to come through the darkness with new insights into the cleansing and healing love of God. Although their dark brushing against our bruised lives can be frightening, they have their use.

Introspection encourages us to look deep inside ourselves to find the answers to current problems. Memories of past hurts or losses revive the pain of grief. We compare our current coping with past responses. We try to make sense of who we are by examining carefully who we have been. The problem is that memories can be distorted. We might see what we want to see. Sometimes we will see things in a less favourable light than they deserve. At other times we will have given them glory they did not deserve. Seeing things and people for what they are is hard work and those who are weary cannot always do that unaided. Memories are a rich source of data that tell us about ourselves: and they are ours!

I like to think of the memory as being like one of those cabinets with glass doors that one sees in many homes. Looking into the cabinet tells me a lot about the occupants of the house and those with whom they have shared their life. A souvenir china cup and saucer might tell me that they had been married at least twenty-five years. A certificate citing their son would tell me that he had once been a first-aider. A campaign medal tells me that someone in the house had served in the armed forces.

The china cabinet does not only contain the whole and the valuable. It contains the little vase lying in fragments, waiting for someone to glue the pieces back together. The whole vase is there. It is just that it does not look like a vase. It did once and the owner can still see how it was the day it was bought. The owner genuinely believes that one day, it will be restored. It is just a matter of getting round to doing it.

In the cabinet is the pottery dinosaur: the result of half a term's work by a 6 year old. It is quite the ugliest dinosaur you can imagine. But then, perhaps all dinosaurs are ugly! It is precious only because it was made by the 6 year old, given in love and placed there with pride. Each item in the cabinet is part of a story. Not all is beauty. Not all is ugliness. Not everything is whole. Some things are tarnished, broken, faded. All are precious.

When we spend some time with our 'friend' Introspection, we are encouraged to open the doors of our 'china cabinet' memory and to take out an item. All items are equally accessible. We can choose. We may be encouraged by God in making our choice. We choose not only the perfect and the whole. We take out the dinosaurs and the medals that speak to us more of battle wounds than of victory. We take up the pieces of broken glass and ponder on how that vase might be restored. As we take an inventory of the contents we reflect upon our life.

I have often wondered how Saint Peter might have reflected on his own life. He might remember the day he was called away from his work as a fisherman or perhaps he would remember the time that he denied that he knew Jesus. I hope he did remember that, but I hope that, in remembering that awful time, he no longer winced at the remembrance of his words and actions. Sometimes it is easier to remember the times we failed: the times we got it wrong. So often we are remembered for our faults rather than for our achievements.

In one church dedicated to St Peter[1] there is a large and brightly coloured east window. The stained glass design is made up of symbols associated with St Peter, and there, in the middle, in all his glory, is a cockerel: the symbol of St Peter's shame.[2] The chains that fell off miraculously are there; the boat, of course, and the fishing nets, but right in the middle, as bold as brass: the cockerel. It is the symbol of Peter's three-fold denial, the three-fold distancing of Peter from his Master. It is the memorial to the moment of moral weakness that seemed to wipe out the occasions of boldness and courage, like the time when Peter took the sword to defend his Master in the Garden of Gethsemane or the bold and impetuous moment when he dared to walk on water. The upside-down cross is there, symbol of the gruesome death that was to befall Peter, but nothing is allowed to take the eye away from that cockerel.

As St Peter looked back over his life, I hope that he remembered not only the sound of the cockerel's mocking crow, and the courtyard fire around which he warmed his shaking hands, but that he remembered too, that meeting on the beach, after the resurrection of Jesus.[3]

I hope he remembered the day that Jesus built a charcoal fire and cooked fresh fish and little loaves of bread on it. Can't you just smell the fire; the food; the sea air? I hope that Peter remembered that delicious breakfast and the conversation with Jesus afterwards. Having given his disciples breakfast, having met their physical needs, Jesus took Peter aside and healed him. He wasn't sick. He wasn't blind. He wasn't lame. He wasn't a leper. When Jesus took Peter on one side he saw in him the redeemed Peter: the perfected Peter; the healed Peter. He saw the whole and the holy Peter. This is what Jesus sees in us.

Healing wasn't mentioned. There was no laying on of hands. Jesus, in three questions, eliciting three responses, healed Peter of all that had gone before. The awfulness of that betrayal the night before Jesus died was taken away. Away went the doubt, the fear, and the confusion. The cockerel was sent away all feet and feathers!

Jesus did not ask Peter if he had faith. Jesus knew he had faith. Peter had been the first to cry: 'You are the Christ, the Son of the Living God.' Jesus simply asked: 'Peter, do you love me?' For it is love that is the key to healing, not faith. And great love is born out of great forgiveness.

It is love, burning in the heart, that touches the compassion of Jesus the Healer. Three times Peter denied Jesus. Three times Jesus invited him to affirm his love: 'Do you love me?' On that fateful night, Jesus had turned and looked at Peter. It was a look of compassion, and love; of sorrow and love; of understanding, and love. It was a look Peter would not forget.

Once again, on the beach of the barbecue breakfast, Jesus looks into Peter's eyes and sees genuine love, a burning love, a zeal which will carry Peter half-way across the world and to his own martyrdom. For this is an encounter with the Christ who is the same yesterday, today and tomorrow. Jesus knew Peter's past with all its failings and Jesus knows his glorious destiny.

There might have been no time at all between the look of the passion and the look of restoration. When it comes to healing our memories, chronological time means nothing. All our memories are equidistant from the *now* moment. Whether something happened ten years ago or ten minutes ago, both can be recalled with the same speed. We are so rich in our memories. *All* our memories are on hand to be of service to us.

The ability and desire of Christ to heal the past is an intrinsic part of his message and of his mission. Christ is outside our time constraints. He can go back and heal the events of the past. In healing those past hurts, Jesus does not wipe them away. He takes them, he transforms them, so that they have value to him and to us. He inspires us to summon a memory. We pick that memory up, we look at it, feel it, smell it, dust it off and we *remember*. We pick up something long forgotten or hidden, and sometimes slowly, sometimes painfully, Jesus heals that hurtful memory. He doesn't say: 'Throw that in the bin.' What he does is to transform that memory. He heals the hurt, and *retains* the memory.

Christ the Healer chooses the place and the time to heal our memories. We have the opportunity to allow Christ to pick out that which *he* wants to heal. He picks it out of the 'china cabinet' of memories. We can let Christ bathe it, restore it, renew it, transform it and then, just as gently and lovingly, put it back. It has its place among the rest of the treasures.

Looking back on our life we can see the hand of Christ the Healer upon us and can marvel at all he has done and continues to do in our lives. Our life is a journey from egocentricity to Christocentricity. Introspection, far from being self-indulgent, need not be a deep well into which we fall, but a tunnel through which we crawl until a dot of light appears in the darkness and gives us hope.

The twin to Introspection is Unworthiness. It too brushes against our lives in a sinister way but it can also have a cleansing effect upon us.

My wife and I once went house hunting. We looked at two adjacent houses on a small estate. The owners of both houses had laid out the rear gardens in a pleasant way. Both could point proudly to the lawn and the shrubs. One owner had spent a lot of money on paving the patio. The other owners explained, apologetically, that they had made their patio from broken slabs bought cheaply at the local garden centre. The expensive patio was smart and neat. The inexpensive one had been carefully laid out, each piece carefully placed against its neighbour. It was full of colour and variety. It looked welcoming and informal. There was no need to apologise. This was one instance where brokenness had the edge. In this instance 'crazy paving' made complete sense.

The owners' problem was that they saw only the brokenness and not the wholeness. They had seen the stones as they arrived from the garden centre. They could recall the bargain offer and had selected from the heap of rejected stone the pieces that would harmonise so well in the finished patio, but they failed to see the beauty of it. It was not, to their mind, worthy of praise.

Part of the problem for us weary people may be that when we look at our own worth we see all the cracks and imperfections and presume they make us less valuable. When we are healed we expect to be invisibly mended. I am sure that God sees us so and that our resurrection self will be without spot or blemish but, this side of heaven, we carry the marks of our healing even as the resurrected Christ carried the marks of the nails in his hands and feet and the mark of the lance in his side. If we were without blemish it might be assumed that we had never sinned or never been in need of healing. As it is, we testify by our mends and joins to the miracle of healing.

In the story of Naaman in the Old Testament,[4] or in the healing stories in the New Testament, those healed would tell their family and friends what happened. Those who knew them blind, lame, or disfigured would see the difference.

Later, they would meet people for the first time and they would find it difficult to appreciate the magnitude of the grace of God since they would see no sign of the former condition. Inward and outward scars are not for us a lasting condition: they will fade as we journey along the eternal continuum. In the meantime we bear the scars of our sins with pride and with gratitude to our Healer King. They tell the story of what we were and what we have become through his love.

Failure to grasp this reality may be the reason why many people carry with them a burden of unworthiness. The weight of that burden may be the cause of their weariness. Knowing our faults and remembering our past sins, now forgiven and redeemed, is all well and good, provided that we do not lose sight of God's love and mercy. We should not lose sight too of the prospect that even as we dwell on our brokenness, God is making something new of us, the glory of which is yet to be revealed in us.[5]

I once watched a potter at work. He hardly noticed the steady stream of people who wandered into his workshop and stood, for the most part silent and transfixed, as he worked the clay. His concentration was absolute. One sensed that he saw in his mind's eye the finished pot. He knew what he was creating. The wheel turned in a rhythmical way as his foot worked a treadle. His foot moved in time with typical human respiration, about twelve to sixteen times each minute. It was easy to breathe with the rhythm of his work and the effect was calming.

The potter's hands were large and firm yet he needed a gentle touch if the clay was to respond under his fingers. He 'threw' one pot and was not satisfied with it. It became distorted and off-centre. The open mouth of the pot yawned and grimaced. He cut the clay from the wheel and set it aside. After adding some more clay and a little water, he kneaded the clay with his knuckles and palms and then, rolling it into a ball, he began again. The pot rose under his fingers. He gave it capacity and shape. He gave it height and texture. Finally he made a spout and added a handle. He removed from the wheel a perfect jug. After firing and glazing it might be sold in the shop next door. It would be used to pour out its contents, perhaps for many years. It might become an heirloom: precious to its owners and their descendants.

My thoughts turned to the prophet Isaiah,[6] to the Lord's poetic words to Cyrus the Ruler, in Babylon, which leave us in no doubt as to who is in charge. The Lords asks if the clay questions what the potter is making of it. In strong terms the Lord makes the role relationships clear: he, the creator God, the Potter; we, the clay, the work of his hands.

The inanimate clay being moulded into a pot does not ask the potter what he is making but we do ask God what he is making of us, even though we might feel guilty about asking. We know that we should trust him completely for he knows what is best for us. If we believe there is a plan for us, it must be God who holds that plan in the palm of his hand, even as the potter holds the clay. 'For I know the plans I have for you,' says the Lord. 'Plans for welfare and not for evil, to give you a future and a hope.'[7]

Wanting to know what God is doing with us is quite natural and human. As clay in the hands of the Potter we may feel as though we are whizzing round on the Potter's wheel: disoriented, frightened, bewildered. As we are moulded under the hands of the Potter we may experience the pain of dislocation, relocation, and change. It is natural that we should cry: 'Lord, what are you making of me? What shall I be?'

When Zechariah questioned the angel who brought tidings

that he was to become the father of John the Baptist, he was punished by being struck dumb until the child was born and named. On the other hand, Mary, the mother of Jesus, was also visited by an angel and told that she was to bear the Emmanuel, the 'God-with-us', the Saviour of the world. She asked: 'How can this be?' She received an explanation in reply to her question. The answer was a mystery. To be told she would conceive by the overshadowing of the Holy Spirit[8] did not bring Mary much closer to understanding but in the question and the answer she established the credentials of the angel and the source of the power behind his message. She was not rebuked or condemned for asking.

In the midst of confusion and at times of change or challenge, we can ask, in sincerity and humility: 'Lord, where is this leading? What are you doing with me? What are you making?' The idea that God is making something of us is healthier than the alternative model, which is to presume that God is 'unmaking' us: breaking us up in anger or retribution. Those who are weary can appreciate fully the breaking and melting part of the process. We need too, to sense the moulding and shaping so that we can co-operate with the Master Potter and minimise our obstruction to his purpose. If we feel only the exhaustion of brokenness without a glimpse at the reassembled vessel we can be further discouraged. We may react badly by kicking and screaming with frustration (two very exhausting occupations). Some will say that to be kept completely in the dark about what God is making provides the ultimate test of faith. I expect they are right, but the God who meets me in my need does not test me without compassion and understanding. He does not test me beyond my strength; I am quite capable of doing that for myself!

The Scriptures tell us that God made us in his image and likeness[9] but we are not clones of God. His image and likeness can take endless forms. If we start from the point of God having made us, perfect and in his image, and then move on to our own brokenness, we may conclude that God is like the potter who makes a pot and, finding it misshapen, throws it against the wall or squashes the clay and starts again. We should not get stuck with this model. It might be more helpful to hold the view that God is the Potter who is moulding the clay. He is the Creator who is creating and recreating us. In the light of our life experiences (both good and bad) he is shaping us into something beautiful and unique, but it is not yet finished. This model allows us to think positively about our experience on the Potter's wheel. Consequently, the pain, the disorientation, the process of change, may not seem so demoralising.

The idea that our suffering is part of God's creative and re-creative work does not stop us protesting about the pain. It has value so long as we can see the point of it. As long as we can sense how the pain contributes to what God is making, we can tolerate it. The reality is that we rarely understand the meaning of our pain, our suffering, or our weariness: at least not at the time. If we do cry out in our anguish or confusion then God will understand why we do that. We have enough evidence of a God of compassion and love to know that he can receive that from us. There will be no rebuke; only compassion. We mean no disrespect. We are not like Zechariah and have no need to be struck dumb. More than ever we *need* our voice, to cry out with. It may be the only release from pain that is available to us.

Those of us who are weary remember when we had the energy to do so much. Now, even basic tasks make such demands. Those who care for us might help us to see who we used to be, and help us to look forward to becoming that person once again. Behind the question: 'What are you making, Lord?' is the question: 'Lord, will I ever be the same as I used to be?' The answer has to be, 'No, you cannot expect to be the same.'

What we discover through pain, doubt, disappointment, anger, and rage, is that God is making something new.[10] He is making it from the person we were and the person we have become. Everything we ever were becomes a component part of everything we ever shall be. Nothing is lost. It takes time to discover the truth of these things and we may be running out of time here on earth. We may have to wait until we get to heaven to see the full radiant beauty of what God is making of us.

Having asked the question of God: 'What are you making?', we declare an interest in the beautiful and the purposeful. We become committed to the outcome. It is a matter of not asking the question if we don't want to hear the answer. The answer may be: 'Come and see.' It is likely to be: 'Come and help.'

God is the creator and the re-creator, but he gives us a share in his re-creative work. Whenever we help ourselves or others, even in a small way, we become partners with God in re-creation. If we are feeling despondent, almost despairing in our weariness, we may not see how we can help ourselves at all. Certainly we cannot do much on our own. We might ponder, however, on what we *can* do.

Our first priority is to do ourselves no harm, since there are many ways in which we may hurt ourselves. They include not taking prescribed medication in the right dose at the right time; not resting when we should; eating an unhealthy diet; not taking exercise when we can. We can do ourselves harm by ignoring advice. Sometimes the harm comes from taking unhelpful advice. I don't pretend that it is easy to discern the one from the other.

Co-operating with the re-creative God may mean a thousand and one things or it might mean one thing only. The individual must decide. If there were one fundamental element to co-operation I would say it was that of adopting a positive mental attitude of openness and readiness to change. When we ask the question: 'What are you making, Lord?' we are already being open and collaborative. We are not accusing the Lord of destroying us or of ignoring our plight whilst we disintegrate. We own that God is making something. We may sense, even for a moment, that he is making of us something beautiful and wonderful. We might experience a flash of excitement and anticipation. It is the flash of a spark of hope that can be kindled into a flame that burns brighter and brighter.

Curiosity is not a sin. Jesus encouraged us to be child-like in our approach to our heavenly Father and curiosity is a child-like quality. It can also be an antidote to destructive and exhausting anger. It is very difficult to be angry and, at the same time, to ask oneself: 'Where did that angry remark come from?'

We need not be afraid to ask: 'What are you making, Lord?' To ask is to be involved and to be a contributor to God's re-creative process. We become partners with the Lord in bringing order out of chaos, wholeness out of brokenness: and thus con-celebrants of a new creation.

References
1. St Peter's Church, Babraham, Cambridgeshire
2. Matthew 26:69-75
3. John 21:9-19
4. 2 Kings 5:1-14
5. 1 John 3:2
6. Isaiah 45:9
7. Jeremiah 29:11
8. Luke 1:26-38
9. Genesis 1:26
10. Revelation 21:5

Focus for reflection

'For I know the plans I have for you,' says the Lord. 'Plans for welfare and not for evil, to give you a future and a hope.' (Isaiah 45:9)

Suggestions for prayer

Dear Lord, help me to remember clearly
    so that I neither glorify a memory
    nor do it an injustice.
Thank you for my memory
    because it is a vast treasure-house,
    a library, a living monument to the life you gave me.
Help me to own my memories,
    both good and bad,
    because they are part of what makes me, me. Amen.

Lord,
    you know the memory I am avoiding;
    give me the courage to choose to look at it,
    touch it, feel it, confront it.

Show me what you wish to heal in me
    at this time.
Bathe me, wash me,
    soak me in your love, mercy, and grace
    so that the pain of that memory is eased away,
    but leave me with the memory now redeemed:
    leave me the scars whilst here on earth
    so that I can show them proudly to others
    as I would battle honours. Amen.

Lord,
    help me to apologise less often
    for who I am. Amen.

Lord, I am too weary to sin seriously
    so don't let me puff up my sins,
    make more of them than they deserve,
    or make more of them than you do,
    lest, out of pride and vanity,
    I make a real sin where there was none. Amen.

Thank you for the gift of curiosity
    which makes me ask you
    what you are making of me.
Help me to be like Mary
    who asked the angel
    how she could become your mother –
    using her gift of curiosity
    without a hint of mistrust. Amen.

Lord,
    show me how I can co-operate with your plans for me:
    plans for welfare and not for evil.
When you send help, advice, treatment,
    teach me to discern your strong yet gentle hands
    moulding me. Amen.

Questions for those alone

Looking back, can you see how the hands of the Potter have shaped you?

Have you dared to ask: 'Lord, what are you making of me?'

Can you trust God with your cries of pain or your anger with him?

Suggestions for group discussion

St Paul tells us that: 'If one member suffers, all suffer together; if one member is honoured, all rejoice together.' How can we bring Christ's healing to each other? How well do we rejoice together?

How can we celebrate what we shall become?

Does the church culture allow people to express their frustrations, disappointments, and anger (with God and with us)?

Chapter 3

The horrors of perpetual day: recovering the value of 'night'

My wife and I, having enjoyed a holiday in the peace and tranquillity of rural France, stayed overnight in Rouen. The hotel was on the corner of a main intersection. In front of it were eight lanes of traffic not including the river and the railway. To the side was an overpass. The whole area was floodlit throughout the night. In addition, cars and lorries thundered past in all directions all night. Headlights were full on; engines roared, pneumatic brakes hissed. Cargoes bounced on trailer-backs, and chassis rattled. The light and noise pollution was incredible. In the early hours of the morning, unable to sleep for the din, it occurred to me that, at last, in the late twentieth century, humankind has conquered the night. Perpetual day has come.

Environmentalists are becoming increasingly concerned about the problems of light pollution. They are gathering evidence from doctors, social workers, teachers, and others about the problems created by continuous exposure to light. It is argued that those who live in our cities are more at risk. Bright street lighting, for instance, is blamed for altered sleep patterns that lower the quality of sleep even if they don't keep one awake. We need some light to enhance safety; other light is used to enhance pleasure, but we may be experiencing our pleasure or our freedom to travel when we wish at the expense of the well-being of others.

We Christian ministers must take some responsibility and own the problem of perpetual day. We must look at how we order our own lives and what we expect of others. I know several clergy who work into the night and then expect to give of their best in the early morning. We must try to restore God's order of creation: the God who created night and day.[1] We must help people to retain night and to value it and not to shun it as negative and bad.

In St John's Gospel[2] Jesus speaks of the work of enlightenment. He is the light that has come into the world and whilst we have the light we must do the work of God. We must do our share of the bringing in of the Kingdom of God. But Jesus, in a play on words, says that 'night comes when no one can work'. That might have been true of his earthly time, but now people can and do work at night.

We would be in a sorry state if the emergency services stopped working at dusk or if essential services were not maintained throughout the night. Clearly not all the work of the night is contrary to the will of God. There are many instances, however, where night working is motivated solely by profit.

To some extent the 'work of the day', the work of enlightenment, is a twenty-four-hours-a-day work. (How many people come to Christ through the ministry of another in the night time? How many of the homeless and the marginalised in our society feel the touch of Christ when hot soup is offered in his name in the middle of the night?) We must not confuse this with a dangerous fusion of two seemingly wholesome Christian precepts. Our slogans read: 'work is good' and 'night is bad'. The key issue, to my mind, is not whether one works at night or during the day but whether or not the balance has been lost; whether or not people are just too busy and whether or not such busyness is always necessary.

The so-called Protestant work ethic came about, as I understand it, as a reaction against sloth and a belief that, as a result of 'the fall', we are condemned to hard labour. Adam and Eve could have had a work-free paradise if they had not sinned and fallen from God's grace. Who was going to prune the trees and weed the Garden of Eden? I do not know. No doubt someone will tell me that weeds, too, are a consequence of the fall. Decadence, sloth and the exploitation of others are anathema to the Christian ethic. Work, which affords opportunities for us to reach our full potential and which maintains self-respect, is my prayer for all.

It can be argued that the Protestant work ethic fuelled the industrial revolution, which has been damaging to health and to family life, but there is no denying that the industrial revolution has brought us many benefits and comforts. This may be the moment to switch on the electric kettle, to make a pot of tea, or to run a hot bath. Whilst soaking in the foamy waters we might reflect on the benefits of modern technology!

Many people in public life proudly boast that they need only a few hours sleep each night and that they can work an eighteen-hour day. They expect similar commitment from those they employ. Lack of sleep and long working hours has broken the health of many. It has broken up marriages and destroyed families. Some research on sleep disorders found that a typical night's sleep has declined in the United States of America by a staggering twenty per cent, with consequent losses in productivity and other human tragedies ensuing.[3]

We call the disease 'workaholism'. We trace its aetiology back through individualism, through commercialism, through to the industrial revolution, to the advent of the Protestant work ethic. It is with a certain irony that we Christian ministers are now promoting quiet days and retreats. Typically, the minister bids the congregation sing, 'Be still for the presence of the Lord' as he scurries around looking for his copy of the hymn book and his sermon notes that he has left in the vestry. As he breathlessly sings the final verse, his mind is full of the names of the people he must remember to include in the bidding prayers later in the service. Regrettably, what we preach and what we do are often quite different.

In an article by Sarah Meyrick in *The Church Times*,[4] Dr George Carey, Archbishop of Canterbury, is quoted as saying: 'I get up early, and that's important. I'm up before six, which may not be very early for some, but we do go to bed very late.' It read like an apology and a justification. In different words and in different ways I hear the same from fellow clergy and others. They are burdened with guilt because they cannot give more hours to their ministry. They should not apologise for needing a certain amount of sleep, as the amount we require is personal and individual. No one can lay down norms for someone else nor should we make others feel guilty if their sleep and rest requirements are greater than ours. My fear is that historical and contemporary role models in the Church, whilst encouraging many, can inadvertently marginalise others. Among them are the weak, the elderly, the frail, the weary and the chronically ill. The reasons vary but they all have the same devastating effect.

It seems that physically, emotionally and spiritually, the Church undervalues the night experience and puts too much emphasis on searing light. We promote an instant change from night to light, which not only devalues night but allows for no shades or shadows of transition. It seems that 'night' is such bad news that we ought to do away with it altogether. We might be tempted to think that by irradiating night, we can remove doubt, disbelief, adversity, affliction or death. The implication seems to be that if we remove night there can be no more night-time thinking. Daylight means work. Feverish activity obliterates soul-searching reflection, which is the core activity of night both metaphysically and metaphorically.

Wrestling with this problem I turned to the Scriptures for inspiration and, according to my concordance,[5] there are approximately 178 references to 'night' in the Bible. My concordance identifies, very helpfully, several uses of the word. The first usage is simply a reference to the sun having sunk below the horizon. If you are reading this chapter after dark, then you have only to look out of the window to know that it is night. You know that your current experience of night is not universal but local and not permanent but temporary. This is crucial to a positive understanding of a metaphorical or spiritual experience of night. We can tell ourselves that although we experience 'night' it is not necessarily a permanent experience. The first 'value' it has is its transience.

I know many people who live with chronic depression, who have learned to remind themselves that although they are feeling low currently, they may not feel low tomorrow or next week. Part of coping with this debilitating illness is allowing that a current mood is likely to be transient. I hear them say: 'Today I feel 40 per cent, tomorrow I may feel 60 per cent. I may never feel 100 per cent again but 60 per cent is bearable. I can live with it.'

A second usage of 'night' in the Bible is for a time of ignorance and unbelief. St Paul, in his letter to the Romans, urges: 'Always remember that this is the hour of crisis; it is high time for you to wake out of sleep, for deliverance is nearer to us now than it was when first we believed. It is far on in the night; day is near. Let us therefore throw off the deeds of darkness and put on the armour of light.'[6] Paul reminds his fellow Christians that they must be up and doing the work of the Lord. There is not a moment to be lost. The old age is passing, the new age is upon us. Up, out, and at it chaps! Perhaps, having written that, Paul paused to reflect on his own life and recalled that, after his dramatic conversion, he was blinded, inactive, and in the dark for three days.[7] Arguably, these three days were as formative as his light-bathed conversion.

In our eagerness for conversion, in ourselves and in others, we need to learn how to value the darkness and our dependency on those God sends to our aid. We need to develop a mindset which allows that the darkness may clear at any time but which also allows that our 'three days' may be a metaphor for a longer period of time over which we have little or no control. The God of grace who speaks in the blinding light is the same God of grace who comforts and nourishes us in the dark; who helps us bear the hidden expense of discipleship. It is the same God who enables us to grow and grow until we are filled with light and expansive purpose.

In Romans 13:11-12, Paul reminds me of myself preparing a sermon in which I want to bring something of the urgency of the Gospel message to the congregation. I want to fire the congregation up with enthusiasm; I want to raise the banner and say: 'Come! Let us get up and go and bring in the Kingdom.' It is a kind of Father Henry V down at St Agincourt's! The words flow, the Scriptures are behind me. I think of the people. I see their faces brighten. I see the 'keenies' sit up and take notice. They nod to each other. 'This is the stuff,' they say. 'Now, at last, we are on our way.'

Then I think of other faces in the same congregation. Not just the tired, the distracted and the dispirited, but those whose faith is not strong at this time. They, too, have come to the Lord. They have touched the hem of the garment of Christ but, just now, their faith is less than certain. They try to conceal their current state because they are ashamed or feel guilty. It could be any one of a number in any congregation. Her neighbour beams at her and says: 'Isn't the Lord good?' She replies, a little too readily: 'Yes, brother, praise God.' However, the inner face is crestfallen. She *knows* that the Lord is good; she can sing 'his goodness faileth never' along with the rest, but she cannot see the goodness just now, because it is night. She may know that the light shines somewhere and that it will shine again for her. This is not the moment to wake and to get up and go. In the darkness she will simply stumble about and take the wrong turn. Maybe, when she came to faith, she had been given glib answers which she was willing to accept at the time. Since then challenges have come and crises have occurred. The answers do not satisfy and she is confused as to which questions it is important to ask.

Working in the dark may produce unreliable results. It is not the time to make life-changing decisions unless they force themselves upon us. Making decisions helps one to feel in control and those in the dark often need to feel that something is within their control. The comfort for those who make decisions in the dark is that they will not always be disastrous decisions. People may even regard them as having been insightful and profoundly significant. Those in the dark need others to be patient, both with their indecisiveness and with any disastrous decisions they make.

People experiencing the 'night' of unbelief or ignorance need the gentle touch. For them, Paul is right. This is the hour of crisis, but far from waking out of their sleep they want desperately to put their head under the bedcovers; and to sink into oblivion from an overdose of self-administered carbon dioxide. I call it the 'Duvet Syndrome'. The rallying call does not make them sit up. It does not make their feet itch to spread the beautiful Gospel of peace. They feel no peace. They see the knowing glances between the 'keenies' and they could be sick.

The message to pastors, preachers and teachers is to be discerning when it comes to making the rallying call. We need to know when to give people permission to stand down for a while and we need to learn how to sit with people until dawn: until waking, walking, and working becomes possible once again. We need to resist the temptation to hurry such people along and to make decisions for them. They too may be hoping that others will take the burden of decision-making from them. Helpers and supporters, both professional and informal, need to learn when it is appropriate to carry the burden of decision-making for someone, and when to encourage them to set the burden aside until they are able to carry it for themselves.

A third usage of night in the Bible is that of adversity and affliction. I spent some time nursing at night. In the winter it was possible to come off duty in the morning and to go to bed while it was still dark. I could go for a week without seeing daylight or feeling fresh air on my face. Perpetual night can have a strange effect on people. Nutritionists tell us we need vitamin D from the sun. Without it we become listless and zombie-like. Those suffering from long-term spiritual or emotional night will need the nourishment of kindness, gentleness and patience.

Although a hospital takes on a whole different atmosphere at night, it can be as busy as it is in the daytime. Carers and sufferers alike have so much to do, even in the dark of night. It is not a passive time. Anyone who has been a hospital patient will know that a good night's sleep is a rarity. Even if *you* can sleep, the patient in the next bed or across the ward may not sleep.

Adversity and affliction take on a whole new meaning. Pain can seem worse; noises are exaggerated; images are distorted; sensitivities are heightened. For some, night-time is a time to think things through. It is the only time to think. It is a time to assess one's situation, to review priorities, to make plans. It can also be the time when things look particularly bleak. Problems seem insurmountable and morale is at its lowest. Hope gives way to despair.

Night carers do not encourage their patients to wake up and to shake off the night, but rather to rest because the body, mind, and spirit need the night for recuperation. The 'night' experience of adversity and affliction cannot be tackled whilst people are fatigued, disoriented and sedated.

A friend[8] once discussed with me the situation where one is adopting what he calls 'middle of the night thinking' in the middle of the day. It is a time when the distortions and the subjectivity of the night are daytime realities. It is a time when one is experiencing 'night' perpetually: a kind of night-time wakefulness or a daytime somnambulance.

This is distinct from (but not so far from) an experience of spiritual night-time which might be more akin to the 'dark night of the soul' described by St John of the Cross, the great sixteenth-century Spanish mystic. He writes of the passive night of the spirit in which we experience the apparent absence of God and the consequent desolation. He sees this as a sign of spiritual growth towards union with God wrought through passivity rather than activity. The writings of St John of the Cross might make us feel that such spiritual heights are beyond us; the eloquence of his words may give the experience described an aura that obscures it and makes it seem out of our reach. We may say of ourselves that we are neither mystics nor saints. We might then assign our night-time restlessness a lower place, giving it much less significance. In reality the two are not so far apart. In both there is an absence of light and often without any logical reason. We do not know why we are 'in the dark' or why the answer to our questions eludes us. In both, we long for the light, or dread the light or both.

Just as the night nurse might treat symptomatically the things that are treatable, so we must treat this daytime night experience in the same way. We ask ourselves the questions she would ask us or herself: 'Are you in pain? Can this pain be treated? Can anything be done, now, to relieve this anxiety? What will bring comfort or distraction until the time is right for a more stable solution? I cannot resolve this on my own. Whom should I call for help?' Put another way, we may find it helpful to ask ourselves: 'What is the best gift I can give myself right now?'

The third value of the night experience is that it is a time for growth. Hair, fingernails, yes! But spiritual growth too. It is not a growth we can burden people with. We cannot say to someone experiencing the pain of affliction that this is doing them some good. Quite often it isn't, but sometimes, and later on, the sufferer can look back and see that they have grown through affliction.

The fourth use of the word 'night' is as a metaphor for death. Spiritual death is caused by serious sin and the reader may have explored this subject in an earlier chapter. It may be sufficient here to make an association between sin and the deeds of darkness. One story from Chapter 13 of St John's Gospel may help to illustrate this and to pull together all the other themes of 'night'. At the Last Supper, Jesus, seeing what was in the heart of Judas, tells him to go and do what he has to do. In verse 30 John records: 'And it was night.'

Imagine how this story was first told around the camp fires of the early Christians. When the story-teller reached the dark deeds of Judas he would say, perhaps in a half whisper: 'And it was night'. Faces caught by the glow of the camp fire would turn to each other and exchange serious and knowing looks. The whisper would go round: 'And it was night'.

It was not just dark outside. True, the sun had disappeared below the horizon, but this was much more. This was about the deeds of darkness. Judas was in the 'night' of his disbelief and ignorance. For Jesus and his followers this would be the 'night' of adversity and affliction. There would be an end to the active ministry of Jesus for his passion, his passivity, was about to begin. The Light of the world was about to be snuffed out in the 'night' of death. The transient night of suffering gave way to the dawning of salvation for the whole world. The value of the night of death is that it leads to life. 'And it was night.' This little sentence in St John's Gospel is, surely, one of the most powerful and moving in Scripture; encapsulating the whole and wonder-full theology of night.

References

1. Genesis 1:1-5
2. John 9:4
3. Daily Mail, 30 January 1998
4. 27 March 1997
5. *Cruden's Complete Concordance of the Bible,* published by Lutterworth Press
6. Romans 13:11-12
7. Acts 9:1-22
8. Mark Williams, a world expert on depression and suicide, and author of *Cry of Pain*, published by Penguin

Focus for reflection

Weeping may linger for the night, but joy comes with the morning. (Psalm 30:5)

Suggestions for prayer

Lord, you are faithful for ever
    even as night follows day.
Help me to cope with the 'night'
    and hold on to a belief that 'day' will follow. Amen.

Remember me, Lord?
I am the one whose faith is not as strong as others',
    at least, not at this time.
Help me to avoid comparisons
    and to rejoice in the way you have brought *me* to faith.
Help me to hold on in my uncertainty
    and to revisit the times and places
    when I knew your presence in joy and peace. Amen.

Dear Lord,
    as I move wearily about
    in the darkness of despondency,
    help me to negotiate the hazards.
Help me to make good decisions
    if I must make them at all.
Help me to keep things in perspective
    in the middle of the night
    as well as in the middle of the day. Amen.

I have stretched out the day you gave
    because the night-time seems such a waste.
Help me to discover your purpose in giving us night.
Lord, you know I have so much to do.
Demands are made on me every day.
I cannot do less without being neglectful,
    yet help me to sort out priorities
    according to *your* will.
Help me to put you back
    in the centre of the universe
    for I have put myself in your seat
    and I do not know how to vacate it! Amen.

Lord, my name is .... and I am a workaholic.

Questions for those alone

Does joy come in the morning? If not, what can I do to cope better with the 'night'?

What might be the purpose of my current experience of (comparative) darkness?

Could I do less than I do, without neglecting the things that are important?

In what ways to I contribute to the erosion of God-given night?

Suggestions for group discussion

Discuss the phenomenon of 'perpetual day'. What is the group's experience of it? Is it a concern?

Can we share how each of us came to faith or to doubt?

Try sitting together in the dark, and in silence, before offering suggestions of how the 'night' experience might be valued. What can still be done in the dark?

Does the church promote workaholism as well as the need for rest?

Chapter 4

Resting, sleeping, and praying:
a twenty-four-hour relationship with God

For many, rest and sleep are thought to be rewards for good behaviour at the end of a hard day. For others, rest is an intrusion into an otherwise busy and fulfilling life. People speak of having to schedule rest times, and although they take them, they do not really rest. They watch the clock and fidget and potter about.

Still others say that they don't rest at all. Instead they do something different from their work activity. They quote the old saying that 'a change is as good as a rest'. A colleague of mine is incensed by the absurdity of that saying. He says that a change is just a change, and no rest at all.[1]

Some have said that a period of rest is an investment in the quality of their life activity. It is an opportunity to reflect and to be renewed. Time management experts might advise us to invest more resources than we expect into planning to do something. Planning time might easily outstrip execution time. In the same way, rest time needs to be commensurate with activity time. I was once advised that the busier I became, the more time I would need for prayer. The advice turned out to be very accurate. The principle is the same.

I wonder if we could imagine ourselves resting for one seventh of our time and yet this is precisely what the writer of the Book of Genesis wants us to understand about God. God rested on the seventh day.[2] Again I am grateful to my colleague for his observation that what was the seventh and final day for God, was the first day for humankind. God rested after his labours but the first thing that the newly created man and woman were to do was to take the day off![1]

Sleep has been described to me as a necessary evil or as an irritating interlude between important episodes of work. Another described work ('toil' was the word used) as a curse: the consequence of sin and the fall from grace.[3] The same person had great difficulty in taking a rest. She was driven by the guilt of her fallen state. Others referred to sleep as an occasion of sin. Lustful, angry, even murderous dreams were interpreted as evil influences. Periods of sleep were a daunting and fearsome episode between periods of wakefulness.

Those who are weary must develop a positive attitude to rest and sleep if they are to make the best use of the energy they have. The reader may want to distinguish between wakeful rest and restful sleep.

God created us in his image and likeness. God's rhythm is our rhythm. We must breathe as he breathes and rest as he rests. Students of human, non-verbal behaviour will have observed that two people who have developed a close rapport begin to match their gestures and the pitch of their voice. Their breathing becomes synchronised. If we invest in our relationship with God we become synchronised with him. Rest periods and times of sleep become opportunities for this relationship to develop.

There are two ways in which the mechanism of human respiration can illustrate something of our rapport with God. Firstly, the mechanism is essentially beyond our control. The nerve stimulation comes from the brain and although we may have some control over the rhythm and pattern of breathing, we cannot for very long, by an act of will alone, prevent ourselves from breathing. Eventually we will have to breathe; and so it is with our relationship with God: we cannot shut him out completely.

The second point about the mechanism of human respiration is that it works on the principle that 'nature abhors a vacuum'. When the diaphragm and the muscles of the chest wall contract, the lungs have to expand because of the vacuum between them and the chest wall. We cannot but draw the breath of God into our souls. Only by not breathing can we keep it out permanently. Only death ends unaided respiration. Only spiritual death can end a relationship with God.

We can learn to control our breathing; taking deep breaths in and out. We find it has a relaxing effect. It is a basic exercise in all relaxation classes and in many forms of meditation. It aids the effectiveness of the use of 'mantra'. The famous 'Jesus Prayer'[4] is recited in synchronisation with the acts of inspiration and expiration.

In the same way that we can manage the quality of our breathing, we can learn to manage the quality of our rest and sleep. We can learn how to let God take control of this valuable and sizeable part of our lives. God becomes not just the God of our activity but the God of our inactivity too. At first it is a chore and requires discipline and (in contradiction) hard work! We have to learn to abandon ourselves to rest and to sleep. Then it becomes a means and a time of grace: a gift, a blessing. A rest period or a time of sleep can become an assignation with the Lover with whom we have a growing rapport.

On a purely human level, many experts have written about enhancing the quality of our life by restful sleep. Practical tips for getting off to sleep and for aiding restful sleep are freely available. I recommend a little book by Leslie Kenton called *Sleep Deep*.[5] Among the many practical tips, she suggests using our imagination to recall a favourite place that we associate with relaxation and rest. It might be a beach with waves lapping gently onto the sand. It might be a pine forest or a hill-top view. Christians need not feel threatened by these techniques (and I know some who are). There are so many vivid images in the Bible that we can find something that transports our mind to a restful place.

There are those who will be tempted to reject the notion that we can equate rest and sleep with prayer. Prayer, they will argue, is work. From there they might find that work replaces prayer and then they might cry, in a complete corruption of the original sense: 'Laborare est orare' – the Benedictine motto that exclaims that 'to work is to pray'. How seductive that is! How clever we are at turning the sense to suit our argument! We need only tell ourselves that the work in hand is 'good' work: that it is laudable, useful work, and we can tell ourselves that, hey presto! we have prayed too.

When are we praying and when are we not? So far we have explored (albeit briefly) two possibilities: when we are resting and when we are working.

There are those who like to compartmentalise their lives. They speak of 'my prayer time' or 'my quiet time'. They may be very disciplined about their prayer time and, of course, regular times for attending on God are important and they bring a discipline and a regularity to the day. The danger is that we may treat prayer like making a nightly phone call when we are away from home. Those who demarcate prayer time from other time are then, by their own definition, not praying for the other twenty-three hours or so, until their next prayer time. This feels unsatisfactory. Much more satisfactory to consider such periods as times of explicit prayer within the context of subconscious attending on God at all times.

I find my thoughts going back to formative days with the Community of the Glorious Ascension. I was introduced to the Daily Office, the Prayer of the Church. Periods of meditation, corporate silence, and the daily celebration of the Eucharist completed the framework for growing into the state of continually attending on God.

In my youth I was not been very good at getting up in the mornings and meditation followed by morning prayer at about 6.45 am was a challenge to me. In the winter the chapel was cosy and quiet. The only noises were the periodic groans of the Prior's dog, and my snoring!

I rejected a sitting position for the half-hour meditation period because it was too easy to cuddle up to a stone pillar with one's hands up one's voluminous sleeves and to nod off to sleep. We were permitted to walk about but, having been woken by the brethren on their way to breakfast as they stepped over me in the church porch, I found it too embarrassing to try that stratagem again. I followed the example of most of the brethren and knelt upright with my arms on the chair in front and my head tucked underneath my arm like a dozing pigeon. I slept just as well but felt less slothful, and it was more discreet.

Occasionally there would be a gentle tap on my shoulder to wake me but for no other reason than that my snoring was disturbing the others. Father Peter Ball, the founder of the

Community and its Prior, never once chastened me for failing to stay awake. Later, when I was a novice, he told me I had a special gift for prayer and encouraged me in the practice of contemplative prayer. I don't know about that, but I certainly had a gift for sleep!

He taught me that prayer was not a matter of how much effort or of how much time we put in, but a disposition of the heart. To want to want to pray *is* to pray. The soul that yearns for God, prays to God. Activity and repose in prayer are not contradictory.

St Augustine wrote this in his *Confessions*:

O Lord God, grant us peace, for all that we have is your gift. Grant us the peace of repose, the peace of the Sabbath, the peace which has no evening. For this worldly order in all its beauty will pass away. All these things that are very good will come to an end when the limit of their existence is reached. They have been allotted their morning and their evening.

But the seventh day is without evening and the sun shall not set upon it, for you have sanctified it and willed that it shall last for ever. Although your eternal repose was unbroken by the act of creation, nevertheless, after all your works were done and you had seen that they were very good, you rested on the Sabbath day. And in your book we read this as a presage that when our work in this life is done, we too shall rest in you in the Sabbath of eternal life, though our works are very good only because you have given us the grace to perform them.

In that eternal Sabbath you will rest in us, just as now you work in us. The rest that we shall enjoy will be yours, just as the work that we now do is your work done through us. But you, O Lord, are eternally at work and eternally at rest. You are for ever at rest, because you are your own repose.

For the weary, and especially for the ill, there are other times of enforced repose; more perhaps than they would wish. However and whenever such opportunities for repose occur, they give access to the God of eternal repose. We glimpse the God of repose long before we enjoy the repose of heaven. Now we begin to see what Saint Paul meant about praying without ceasing. Accessing the God of repose through our rest and sleep is as much prayer as attending on the dynamic God of activity.

To use a musical analogy, ways of praying are the melody over the base line of a continuing relationship with God. I once heard a musical ensemble whose instruments comprised two violins, a viola, a cello, a double bass, an accordion and a harpsichord. They played a piece by an eighteenth-century Scottish composer. The cellist and the bass player simulated the sound of bagpipes by maintaining a single and continuous note over which the others played a delightful and evocative melody. Over the base line of yearning for God (unconscious prayer) there is the melody of conscious prayer.

It takes effort to use many of the traditional forms of prayer. The reading of the daily office can be tedious when continually said alone. Making time and space amid the distractions of the world can seem near impossible. We make the effort when and where we can to follow some sort of rule of life and discipline of prayer. My argument, however, is addressed to the weary whom I want to save from the destructive lure of becoming the guilt-ridden weary. My question to them is: 'Do you have a longing, a thirst for God?' If you have a longing for God, even if you feel unable to do much about it, your prayer life is not in as bad a state as you might imagine.

There are many examples of the frail and the elderly who, in former years, have been dynamic and active members of the Church. They have met the demands of their paid employment; they have raised a family and managed a home. Now they are frail. They are less sure-footed. Their memory and concentration are not what they were. They may be suffering from chronic and debilitating illness which thwarts their plans and severely limits their mobility.

They express the anxiety that they can no longer take an active part in the life of their local church and they feel guilty that they can no longer do as much as they used to. Conditioned to think of their prayers in the same way as their other church activity, if they cannot be active in prayer they may feel their praying is non-existent and carry a burden of guilt along with the other burdens of life.

Many spiritual writers would say that the inability to be active in prayer opens the mind and the will to opportunities for passive contemplation. Those who are now inactive are in a privileged position because they can only manage to sit and be still in the presence of the Lord. They may be unaware of the privilege and opportunity for passive contemplation and may need encouragement and help. Even then, they can feel compelled to *do* something. In the Church we have been very good at encouraging people to do things. We have been less helpful when it comes to encouraging people to *be*. Those who have learned to be still after a lifetime of being busy can be an inspiration to us. To sit with them and to share the stillness can be a tonic. They can be for us a reservoir of stillness from which to drink and be refreshed. Not a stagnant pool: more like a pool of still water cupped in a rock in the middle of a gentle waterfall. The flowing water before it testifies to what went before and the continuing waterfall keeps open the possibility of further activity. Others may regard themselves as meagre or inadequate 'reservoirs': no more than a drop of dew sitting in the centre of a lupin leaf in the early morning. Nevertheless, God has filled them with himself.

Those who care can help the weary by setting them free from the guilt they feel because they are no longer active in the life of the Church. The Church is dead without its relationship with God. That relationship is founded on prayer. Prayer, passive and active, is just as valuable as running round the parish, being busy about so many things. It is the story of Martha and Mary.[6]

By contrast, consider the example of Richard. I was asked to lead a multi-denominational Lenten study group. Everyone in the group was known to each other. They had met at the same venue in previous years. By the third week in Lent, it became obvious that this year we had been spending a little longer in prayer and reflection.

On the fourth occasion, I suggested we might like to spend five minutes in silent prayer and everyone agreed. A candle was lit and the room lighting subdued. I had no sooner announced the beginning of the five minutes of silence than Richard began to pray aloud. It went something like this: 'O Lord, we thank you that we can just come before you in silence and just be in your presence and know that you are just here to just minister to us in the silence of our hearts and that we have no need to say or do anything but just to let you speak to us . . .' Richard prayed aloud like that for the full five minutes.

There is a fear among some Christians that silent prayer and openness to the ministry of the Lord is dangerous. A blank space is a gap in the defences, into which a thousand demons may rush and corrupt the soul. At least, that is how it has been expressed to me. If I have misunderstood, please forgive my ignorance. Can the soul that yearns for God be so vulnerable in a moment or two of silence, during a period of rest, or during a few hours of sleep?

Many have written most ably about distractions in prayer and on how to meditate. For those who are ill, anxious, or weary for any reason, the distractions may be caused by worry, pain, fear or guilt. These cannot be spirited away as if they were demons that distract from prayer. They *are* the prayer. To paraphrase some words of Jesus: 'Even if I were to keep silent, my aching bones or my aching heart would cry out for me.'[7] To whom can they cry but to the Lord, whose aching bones were stretched over the cross like an animal skin left to dry in the heat of the sun?

Once we let go of the idea that prayer is something we *do* and realise that it is something we *are*, the possibilities are endless. The prayer, as relationship with God, has all the potential of any relationship and more. The God who comes to us comes not only when we are strong and brimming over with energy to make the relationship work. He comes when we have nothing to offer; when we are drained of resources; when we are weary.

He comes in the 'night', in every sense that we have explored so far.

In these circumstances we come to realise that prayer is no effort of ours at all. It is the Spirit of God at work in us: in our wakefulness and vigilance, and in our rest and sleep, in sighs too deep for words.[8]

Waking or sleeping we become increasingly conscious of the God of activity and the God of repose. We develop another sense that utilises all our senses. Perhaps we call it the numinous: a sense of the awe and wonder of God, of his enveloping presence.

It may be helpful to explore the link between numinous and heightened sensual awareness, which is a feature of so many illnesses. Although hypersensitivity can be a burden to us and to others, it can be an experience of heightened sensual awareness, and a time when we can discover the presence of God.

During my nursing career and in parish ministry, people have shared an experience of the God who came in the night. Whether the night was actual or metaphorical is irrelevant. They spoke of the person who made them more comfortable when none of the staff had been near them for some time. They spoke of the person who sat next to them on the edge of the bed and who kept them company. In reality there had been no visitors and all the other patients in the ward were bed-bound. They told of words of comfort or encouragement they had heard when no one had spoken. I have written 'in reality' when I have no right to do so. Those who have known the comfort of the presence of God have touched Reality. Rationality, logic and reason have lower priority.

The rational explanation is that such people were hallucinating, maybe due to medication or toxicity. Perhaps they were dreaming. The Scriptures and the lives of the saints tell us that another explanation is possible. We have a God who cares about us and who may be called 'Absent' at times, but at other times he is called 'Present'. Heightened senses of hearing and sight bring unwelcome noises and images but they can also bring inner sight and inner hearing which is awareness of the presence of God.

References

1. The Revd Tony Treen, Rector of Walpole St Peter, etc.
2. Genesis 2:2
3. Genesis 3:17
4. The Jesus Prayer. A monologue prayer dating from the fourth century AD, and originating in the Eastern tradition: In its standard form it runs:
   Jesus Christ, Son of God, have mercy on me.
   (Kallistos Ware writing in *A Dictionary of Christian Spirituality*, edited by Gordon S. Wakefield, published by SCM.)
5. *Sleep Deep* by Leslie Kenton, published by Health and Beauty
6. Luke 10:38-42
7. Luke 19:40
8. Roman 8:26-27

Focus for reflection

I will both lie down and sleep in peace;
for you alone, O Lord, make me lie down in safety. (Psalm 4:8)

Suggestions for prayer

Lord, I do not know how to pray.
Pray in me to the Father
    through the deep indwelling of your Spirit.
Use my senses to bring me truly alive
    to your creation and to your presence. Amen.

Lord of the night,
    who comes to minister to me in my anguish,
    let me sip the cup of your sustaining love:
    let me drink deeply of your compassion.
Lord, I cannot sleep.
In my wakefulness, keep me calm.
Keep far from me the spectres that haunt the darkness
    and grant me a sense of your abiding presence
    keeping watch with me.
Grant me the gift of sleep. Amen, amen, amen, amen, amen.

Be with me, Lord, in the Advent of my life
    as I long for your return and ponder on your abiding.

Be with me in the Easter of my heart
    as I lose my passion in yours
    that I may rise in glory with you. Amen.

The reader might try what I call 'the prayer of the lap of the Lord':

As you lie down to go to sleep you may have brought to bed with you your worries, your pain, your despair, your guilt of things left undone or handled badly. As you lay your head on your pillow, imagine that you are kneeling at the feet of the Lord seated by you. Imagine your head resting on his lap. Smell the linen of your pillow and smell the Lord's garment. You have come to touch the hem of that garment, to find his strength, his healing, his forgiveness, and his peace. Bring to him all that weighs you down and feel the weight of your head on his lap. Don't fear that your weight is too much for him to bear. Remember he took the weight of the sins of the world upon him. Rest now and ask him for the gift of sleep. You have not stopped praying. Hopefully you will doze or sleep. You may not wake refreshed but you need not add to your troubles the anxiety that you have not prayed.

Lord, I am too weary to pray in words just now.
Let me commune with you in the night.
Hold me close to you and let me sleep in you. Amen.

    I heard the voice of Jesus say:
    'Come unto me and rest;
    lay down, thou weary one, lay down
    thy head upon my breast.'
    I came to Jesus as I was,
    weary, and worn and sad;
    I found in him a resting-place,
    and he has made me glad.
    H. Bonar 1808-89

Questions for those alone

How do you feel when you are too weary to pray?

Is your tiredness a prayer in itself?

Are you too weary to sleep? What might you do to overcome the problem? Who might help you?

When you are weary, are you hypersensitive to images or sounds? Do they distract you from God or do they make you more conscious of him?

Think back. Have you known God as 'Absent' as well as 'Present'?

Suggestions for group discussion

How do we regard rest and sleep? How much sleep is enough?

Share ideas for getting effective sleep and for creating opportunities for periods of rest.

Does the idea of a 'twenty-four-hour relationship with God' change your understanding of both prayer and rest?

Chapter 5

'My yoke is easy, my burden light':
on motivation

I saw a boy of about 4 years of age emerging (with his parents) from a local toy shop. He was carrying an enormous box containing a train set. He could barely stagger along with it. His parents offered to help but he would not let them. The excitement and joy showed in his face. He could not wait to get home to rip open the box and to set up the train set. Mundane things like food, drink, or sleep were, presumably, a long way from his mind.

A few days later, I saw the same boy with his mother, emerging from a supermarket with a trolley piled high with groceries. The mother asked the boy to carry a box of cereal which was sliding off the top of the trolley. As I walked behind them I heard the boy protesting and grumbling that the box was heavy and awkward. He asked why his mother could not have bought a smaller one or made room for it on the trolley. He wanted to know why she had parked the car so far from the door. As I overtook them both I saw the boy's face. Gone was the smile of a few days before. Gone was the excitement and anticipation.

These two incidents set me thinking about motivation and about the words of Jesus: 'My yoke is easy and my burden light.'[1] The whole text is worthy of reflection. 'Come to me all who are weary and whose load is heavy; I will give you rest. Take my yoke upon you, and learn from me, for I am gentle and humble-hearted; and you will find rest for your souls. For my yoke is easy to bear, my load is light.'

Maintaining motivation in the face of chronic weariness is, in itself, a wearisome occupation. We look around us at all the things we ought to do. We might fantasise about doing them all, but we do none of them because the magnitude of them demotivates us. I remember a young theology student addressing a suburban congregation about the needs of the people of their city.

He spoke of the problems of the homeless, and of substance abuse. He spoke of the plight of the unemployed; of battered wives and of abused children. He suspected the congregation were complacent and his aim was to motivate them into action. He had the reverse effect. He asked the congregation to give him some 'feedback' from his sermon and they did. It was not what he expected. Many said that they felt so overwhelmed by the enormity of the social problems he described that they were inclined to feel that they could do nothing. Had he highlighted one problem and perhaps suggested a small way that they could help, they may have responded and gone beyond his expectations.

Being overwhelmed by the 'all' that needs doing can prevent us from doing anything at all; yet we cannot leave everything to others. I don't imagine that there is an occupation in the world that does not have its uninspiring chores. Mostly we accept this aspect of an occupation, perhaps because there are other aspects of it which are fulfilling. When the occupation is all chore and no fulfilment it can be difficult to get out of bed to go to work. Most employers will testify to the high sickness and absence rates among employees who are poorly motivated, frustrated or unfulfilled in their job. I was once accused of only enjoying the things I was good at. Enjoying the things we hate to do is asking rather much. We learn to accept what has to be done, even when there is no motivation to do it. We console ourselves with the tasks that generate new energy in us. In short, we learn to accept what we cannot change, but we need to distinguish between acceptance and resignation. Acceptance which we have worked towards and achieved can, in itself, be fulfilling. Resignation leaves us with a demotivating and de-energising burden.

My concern is illustrated by the story of an immigrant farmer who left his family, culture, and homeland to live in another country. He worked all his adult life in a factory with no view of the hills or fields. There was no fresh air to invigorate him, only the smell of grease and oil. The motivation for moving might have been a basic need to find an income to feed himself and his family. He may have left home so that there was one less mouth to feed. He might say, after thirty years' work, that he is reasonably content with his lot. He has settled for what was real. He might say he still misses his homeland or another way of life but he has come to terms with the reality of his situation. He has married and has had a family. He belongs to a number of clubs and an expatriate association. He has become an active member of his local church. Why would I be concerned for such a man? One might envy his life.

Listening to this story we might just hear the wistfulness, and, behind the contented face, we might discern a longing for something different or something more. Should we say to that man: 'Be content with what you have. You have much more than many'?

Over the years he has shouldered and experienced loss. He has lost contact with the soil he knew. He has lost sight of the fields and he has lost the sound of silence. He has shouldered new burdens of prejudice against the incomer. Should anyone lay upon him a burden of guilt about his continuing aspirations for 'the old country' and the things he has lost? He may, if he can, leave those aspirations to one side but I don't think anyone else can tell him he ought to do so.

His aspirations have been, from time to time, the one thing that has got him out of bed in the morning. The sum total of his ambitions is more than bread on the table and a fire in the grate. His weariness after a long day doing a job he really dislikes is helped, not only by the warmth of his fireside and the food in his belly, but by the photograph albums, now shabby and faded, that rekindle the memories and stir the longing. No one can say to him: 'Burn those. This is your life now. Be content.'

The pious advice to him might depend upon which century he lives in. It might depend upon which continent he resides in. In my experience the advice falls into one of two philosophies.

First there is what I call the 'jam tomorrow' theology. The emphasis will be on accepting one's lot as inevitable and unavoidable with a promise of eternal bliss. I do appreciate, however, that we shall not be completely content this side of heaven because our homeland is with our loving Father God, and we are, to some extent, in exile here on earth.

Ronald Rolheiser, a Canadian priest, once invited his readers to reflect on the aphorism: 'Life is hard.' He continues: 'Almost everything in our culture invites us to believe the opposite; or at least to believe that if our own lives are hard we are doing something wrong.' He goes on to write that 'so much around us suggests that life should not be hard, but comfortable, devoid of pain, frustration, illness, and loneliness'.

He wants us to accept the fact that life is hard and suggests that, as a result of accepting, we will be a lot less self-centred, impatient and angry with our situation. To add theological weight to his argument, he suggests that, when we are baptised, 'we are signed with the sign of the cross to teach us precisely this'.[2]

When we have experienced something of the cross in our lives, then we know the significance only too well. We also hope to experience the rising of Christ. The acceptance of 'the cross' does not remove an aspiration for 'resurrection'. The writer seems to imply that we stay on the cross, with Christ, and do not rise with him: at least not in this life.

One is reminded of those parts of Christendom where there is great poverty and oppression. The promise of glory in the next world seems to be all the Church can offer. In contrast, some Christians want to free people from the yoke of oppression and want people to experience liberty, justice and equity. The imperative is to bring the whole of the Christ event, the whole fruit of the Incarnation to humankind: passion, cross, and resurrection.

This need not be a political and national aspiration only. There are opportunities every day to relieve pain, and to lift spirits, to make this life less hard, less oppressive, so that we can be set free to experience a little of the resurrection in this life. So often it is the 'hard' things in life that make us self-absorbed and prevent us from looking outward to the needs of those around us; that keep our horizons set low.

Let us stay with the example of pain relief. Thirty years ago, pain control was still in its infancy. Most doctors had limited training or experience is its management. Many were (and still are) afraid to try new ways or new combinations of therapies.

Doctors and nurses would ask patients with chronic unremitting pain to be stoical; to be accepting and to endure that which could not be alleviated. In many instances the failure to manage the pain was down to ignorance or fear, and not down to a lack of scientific or medical knowledge.

The hospice movement showed a different way. In the relief of pain come new opportunities for people to say to their loved ones: 'I love you'; 'Thank you'; 'Forgive me'; 'Do this for me or my children' – expressions of the heart that are 'resurrection' in themselves.

I remember Sarah: a patient in a hospice. She had terminal cancer and she had been very sick for several days (apparently as a result of inappropriate pain remedies). When she arrived at the hospice she looked ashen, clammy, and moribund. Her anxious and distressed relatives were with her, expecting the worst but hoping for the best. Twenty-four hours later Sarah was sitting out of bed. She was dressed and her hair had been combed. She had eaten and drunk a little. She looked out of the window at the blue of the sky between resting comfortably: eyes closed.

This small 'death' had been followed by a small 'resurrection'. If someone had said to her or to her relatives: 'Life is hard: accept your pain, frustration and illness', she may not have had those valuable extra weeks to set her life in order.

The medieval concept of 'laudable pain', thought to have a soul-cleansing effect or to store up merit in heaven, is difficult to support. But if it helps to think of it that way, then it is for the sufferer to decide. It is not for others to expect it. Only the sufferer can surrender to pain, and the possible merits of such surrender have to be weighed against the merits of being relieved of the pain. For some, pain may be all they have. No two people respond to pain in exactly the same way. No one can measure someone else's pain. To say to such a person: 'Accept your lot. Think of the glory to come (jam tomorrow)', is to deprive them of the possibility of experiencing resurrection *now*.

I asked a few weary people to share their reflections on the Zen-like aphorism, 'Life is hard'. They said it brought a mixture of anger and laughter. They *know* how hard life is, and how hard it is to take even tiny steps towards the recovery of self-esteem and a sense of purposefulness. They laughed at what they felt was the most demotivating statement they could imagine.

The second school of pious advice is that of 'jam today'. The weary are harangued by those who seem to have their life sorted out, 'together'. They beam from ear to ear and speak with such confidence about how they have no worries or problems since they welcomed Jesus into their life. For those with reservations about the Christian Gospel; for those too weary even to weigh its message, the effect can be seriously demotivating.

Somewhere between 'jam today' and 'jam tomorrow' lies the reality. It is not a static reality. We are a pilgrim people. We journey but, sometimes, we seem to make no progress. Some-times we seem to be walking up the escalator that is going down: we feel we are getting nowhere at all. Sometimes we have curled up in a ditch at the side of the road and dozed off. How long for? We do not know. At other times we regress or lose our sense of direction. Just occasionally we make a step in the right direction and feel the satisfaction of that. Precisely at that moment, someone may remind us that we have only three million more steps to go and our heart may sink to our boots. What we need at that moment, having circled the desert for what seems like forty years, is for someone to celebrate our progress with us: to celebrate and to help us plan the next step, weighing the pain against the potential for growth in the Spirit.

Presenting the weary with another mountain to climb whilst they are still rubbing their sore feet from the previous upward incline, serves only to disempower them and to demotivate them. The mountain ahead may obscure the sun that might bring warmth and comfort to weary bones. *We* might be the mountain that we bid others to climb over or walk round. It might be the mountain of guilt we pile up in front of the weary when we show them, insensitively, how much better our way of life is (even if it be true). The mountain is called 'hopeless-ness' and the sign says: 'Don't expect to climb this in this life.'

The way forward, for many, is a combination of finding new energy not only for the basic needs of life such as food, shelter, and belonging, but finding energy to address some of the deeper and less easily defined yearnings. Setting realistic goals for ourselves brings a sense of achievement: goals not so ambitious that we set ourselves up for failure and risk fuelling our sense of guilt and self-loathing, but measured steps that give expression to our aspirations whilst accepting the limitations upon us. We need satisfiers that are not just useful and purposeful, noble and altruistic. When everything involves huge effort, not all energy should go into the chores of life. Jesus came that we might have life in its fullness. Some things we do, for others and for ourselves, we should be allowed to do because it delights us to do them. God has done so much for us, not because he needed to but because he delights in us.

If we feel called to walk beside another on their life journey, even for a short distance, we need to assess their view of the road ahead: we need to know how the road feels beneath their feet. We can try to share their 'on-the-road' experience. This will include the 'now' experiences of grace and glory. It will include the serenity of things accepted but we do it in a way that does not compound their guilt and lower self-esteem.

We can share with them our vision of heaven, and share with them our spiritual 'homesickness', not in a way which puts a heavy yoke of guilt around their necks, or adds to their burdens, but in a way which builds hope and energises them, and us.

Let us consider a different sort of 'yoke': the yoke of Christ, and remind ourselves that the yoke of an ox is as much to keep the ox from falling into a ditch as it is to make sure the ox keeps working. The yoke brings a sense of security. The yoke, far from being a constraint, sets us free from so much energy-consuming reflection about which road to take. The Lord steers, we have only to watch our step. There is a partnership to be struck between us and God that allows us to tend the aspirations for the future rooted in our restless hearts as well as the needs of today, without being too anxious for tomorrow.[3]

There remains the issue of 'burden', the burden of Christ. I hear many Christians using this word 'burden' and it puzzles me. They may say to me that they have a burden for me. By this they may mean that I have been in their minds lately and that they are concerned for my welfare. They may describe a burden they have as being an ambition to promote one aspect or another of the Kingdom of God. They may have taken on a particular cause and feel a burden of prayer for it.

So often, however, the burden does not seem light in the way that Jesus said it would be. Our Christian friends seem to want us to know that their 'burden' is burdensome, that it involves them in prayer, fasting, alms giving, letter writing, protesting, mountain moving and a host of other activities. Then, perhaps, having the light burden of Christ himself is a different thing altogether. Are they saying, by their burdened demeanour, that the work of Christ is a heavy burden whereas the person of Christ is not a burden at all? Those interested in exploring the Christian faith might mistake the one for the other. They might conclude, from the way the I-have-a-burden Christians behave, that the words of Jesus are a myth: clearly being a Christian is burdensome. These same Christians will have told us that, since they met Jesus, their burdens fell away from their shoulders, but that is not what one sees or hears. What should we say to those whose incisive observations blow a hole the size of the Channel Tunnel through the inconsistencies of being a Christian and sharing the work of Christ?

This sense of there being a difference between the two came quite clearly to me when a colleague asked after my wife's health. Rose has chronic osteo-arthritis, serious enough for her to be retired prematurely from her nursing career. She is not one to complain, and, consequently, few know how badly the condition affects her. On this occasion, instead of giving a polite and dismissive answer to the enquiry after her health, she told it like it was.

The enquirer's shoulders sank visibly and by at least three centimetres. His face took on a burdened expression and, with a deep sigh, he said that he would add Rose's name to 'the list'.

We understood this to be a list of people for whom he prayed. We were grateful for the offer of prayer but Rose acquired a new burden: that of being concerned that she had burdened another who seemed to have burdens enough already!

I was left wondering how the enquirer's response accorded with the words of Jesus: 'My yoke is easy, my burden light.' The privilege of praying for another came across more like the youngster's packet of cornflakes than the train set.

We cannot take upon ourselves the burden of the sins of the world. Jesus, the Lamb of God, has done that. He has been sacrificed, once and for all. The battle between good and evil makes demands upon us, and by God's grace alone we over-come. The battle between hope and despair commands much of our energy, too, but God supplies all we need. When we endeavour to deny ourselves and take up our cross to follow Jesus, we try to shoulder the burdens that are part and parcel of human existence, and so we should. What we must not do is to turn the joys and privileges of our life into burdens of another kind. By so doing, we are implying that we do not expect to have joy in this life, but only in the next. We seem to turn the joys into a burden so that we can tell ourselves that it is all right to have them.

Jesus also said that we are to come to our Father as little children.[4] As children, the burdens we delight to carry and the burdens with which we fight and struggle might say more about our self-centredness than anything else. As adults we try to shoulder, responsibly, the burdens over which we have no control. Many other things are undertaken voluntarily, but we try to avoid perceiving them as burdensome, and try to avoid imposing them on others.

We carry Christ deep within our being even as he carries us over the fire and the quicksand of life. As we journey, we could do worse than to take the child as our model. We put our trust in Christ. We put our hand in the hand of the Saviour and walk companionably with Christ who is then not burdensome. Compared with the weight of the cross, the Christ-child is no weight at all.

References
1. Matthew 11:28-30
2. Ronald Rolheiser, from an article under his column 'In Exile', *Western Catholic Reporter*, 9 November 1997
3. Matthew 6:34
4. Matthew 18:3

Focus for reflection

Take my yoke upon you, and learn from me,
for I am gentle and humble-hearted;
and you will find rest for your souls.
For my yoke is easy and my burden light.
(Matthew 11:28-30)

Suggestions for prayer

Lord,
I am sinking beneath the weight of all I have to do.
I am finding life very hard just now:
    so much to think about;
    to worry about; to carry about.
Please help me.
At the same time help me to sort out
    which burdens I should be carrying,
    and which I should set down.
Help me to find ways
    to off-load anything I am carrying unnecessarily. Amen.

Lord, I am so concerned for your world.
I am overwhelmed by what I read,
    by what I hear on the radio,
    and by what I see on the television.
I feel helpless in the face of tragedy and strife.
I long to go out there and to do something.
I end up doing nothing because I have come to think
    that I, personally, cannot make any difference.

Help me to think of one small way in which I can help,
    and to focus my attention on it.
Show me how you can use me
    in your plan to transform the world. Amen.

Grant me, Lord, your yoke
    to keep me on the right path.
Prevent me from falling off the path
    and into the ditch;
    especially into the ditches I have dug for myself.
Help me to keep my eyes on the way ahead;
    revive in me the zeal I once had,
    and the longing for new heavens and a new earth.
At the same time,
    keep me in the reality of today
    for this is where I live. Amen.

Lord, thank you
    for the times that you have carried me.
In my heart I know that I carry
    the most precious of burdens:
    and you are no weight at all. Amen.

Questions for those alone

Is there one burden that the Lord may not want you to carry at this time and which he may be asking you to lay down?

When you consider all that is happening in the world around you, is there one small way in which you could make a difference?

If you find it difficult to accept the help of others and feel yourself to be a burden to them, could you consider that you might be their way of making a difference in the world?

Suggestions for group discussion

As a Church, how do we use the expression 'a burden'?

71

Many people feel overwhelmed by their burdens. How can we relieve each other of unnecessary burdens?

The Lord is making new heavens and a new earth. How can we help?

Chapter 6
David and Goliath: focusing the energy

'Management' is a word that sends a shudder down the spine of many a Christian minister. It conjures up images of 'sharp' suits and clipboards. It speaks to them of bureaucracy and administration. In short, all the things that a good pastor disdains because they get in the way of good pastoral care. The reality is that we are all managers. We manage ourselves, our time, our resources: in fact anything our loving Father has put into our hands and for which we are accountable to him. We manage our energy and we manage our fatigue. We manage our health by eating properly or by taking the appropriate amount of fresh air and exercise. We manage our ill health by self-medication or planned rest and exercise. We consider why we are here on this earth – what God wants of us – and as we assess our gifts, talents and life we gladly work out a strategy for the application of all those resources and we try to evaluate the effectiveness of what we do.

A common alternative is that we go about in an uncoordinated fashion, moved by whim from one activity to another. We might call that 'being open to the Spirit of God', but the God I know is a God of order and discipline as well as a God who sets us free. We are free not to be capricious and subjective in all we do, but free to be ordered and disciplined and effective in what we do. A friend once said to me that one cannot be organised and holy as well. I beg to differ.

We do not manage ourselves in isolation. There are experts and specialists around us to advise us on a suitable regimen. Doctors and therapists recommend programmes of treatment. Family members watch over us lovingly, concerned that we do not make ourselves ill from over-work. Spiritual guides help us to steer a course following the navigation of the Spirit of God, and they journey with us through storm and tempest, fire and flood. With the help of others, we can learn to manage ourselves, under God, to his greater glory.

To those who dismiss the notion of strategy and try to claim the higher moral ground by pointing to the cross, I respond by saying that the salvation of the world by our Lord Jesus Christ is the result of the greatest stratagem of all eternity.

Watching a fisherman on the riverbank, one sees that he does not throw the whole of his line into the water at once. He does not bunch the line into a tangled heap like a plate of cooked spaghetti and throw it into the water, hoping that he might catch a fish that way. Rather, he lets his line out a little at a time, taking note of the currents in the water as he senses the play and drift of the line to the spot where he expects to find the fish. Then, when he feels the tension on the line and the pull of the fish, he reels in his catch, being careful not to snag the line on the way. Throwing in all the line at once does not increase one's chances of catching a fish.

Giving all one has might be laudable but giving it indiscriminately is foolish. Yes, we look at the cross and see the price of salvation and we have a desire to emulate the Saviour. In truth we cannot ever hope to do that. We have been given so much by God. Learning *how* to give back to him all that we have in love and service is just as important as having the intention to do so.

God is the supreme strategist and he has shown his servants, in every generation, how to be strategic in his service. We could consider some of the great reformers of the Church, like Teresa of Avila, or St Francis of Assisi whose simplicity cloaks the brilliance of his ability to make the best possible use of God-given opportunities. Knowing just when to strip naked before one's bishop, for the maximum effect, takes all kinds of gifts but timing is one of them!

We need look no further than to the familiar Old Testament stories to give us inspiration. The story of David and Goliath is an example of the value of strategic thinking in the service of God. The contribution of David to the history of the people of God is too great and too significant to describe in this work. Certainly David was someone very special. He had many gifts and personal attributes. Today we would say he was a charismatic person. David is described in the Scriptures as handsome, with ruddy cheeks and bright eyes, but there was more to him than good looks.[1] He was a shepherd: a job which requires total commitment and dedication. It is more than a job; it is a way of life. I have come to know a few shepherds in recent years and I have come to appreciate the range of skills required. Shepherding is both an art and (today) a science. It is more than both to the dedicated shepherd. It is not surprising that Jesus described himself as 'The Good Shepherd'.[2] A shepherd needs to be resourceful and inventive. Shepherding requires patience because sheep can be awkward, stubborn creatures, which wander away and get themselves stuck in dykes and ditches. Unable to free themselves, they require coaxing and encouraging as well as firm handling if they are to be rescued from death. It is not surprising that Jesus likened us to sheep!

David was also a gifted musician. He played the lyre and was engaged by King Saul to soothe him when God sent an 'evil spirit' upon him. Today we might deduce that Saul was suffering from a mental disorder that caused him to have frenzied outbursts.

Saul appointed David to be his armour-bearer, a post that would keep David close to Saul. He would be available to play his soothing music whenever it was required. We are also told that David went to Bethlehem from time to time to tend his father's flock.[3] He managed two jobs at once!

David was on an errand from his father, Jesse. He was sent to his brothers, who had left home to fight in the war against the Philistines. David's task was to take some cream cheeses to the commanding officer, in exchange for information regarding the welfare of Jesse's other sons. David arrived as battle was about to commence. He left his cheeses with the quartermaster and ran to greet his brothers.

It was then that David saw Goliath for the first time. Goliath is recorded as being nine feet high. The Israelite soldiers fell back in fear. Day after day Goliath appeared in front of the Philistine army to taunt the Israelites and to fill them with fear.

David overheard the soldiers talking about the rich reward that King Saul was offering to the man who could defeat Goliath: he was promising his daughter in marriage, and exemption from service due in Israel for that man's family.

As the story unfolds, the writer is keen to contrast the might of the Philistines and their champion Goliath with the youthful, rustic but sensitive, musician. David stands before the King and says: 'Let no one lose heart. I shall go and fight this Philistine.' Saul echoes the contrasts already drawn: 'You are not able to fight this Philistine; you are only a lad, and he has been a fighting man all his life.' Innocence, inexperience and the recklessness of youth are contrasted with manhood, experience and strength.

David leaps to his own defence and describes how, as a shepherd, he has fought and killed lions and bears. For good measure, David says: 'The Lord who saved me from the lion and the bear will save me from the Philistine.' Saul gives David permission to go and fight Goliath. Before we consider David's strategy for defeating Goliath, let us ponder on the circumstances and factors which contributed to David's unique opportunity.

David already had access to the king. If David's lyre-playing did have a soothing effect on Saul then, presumably, David had already found favour with him. He already had the king's ear and the king's attention and he had a legitimate reason for being on the battlefield. His father had sent him to bring him word of his other sons. Access to the battlefield and to the information was through bribery. Nowadays it is difficult to imagine how some cream cheeses would open the right doors. Bribes and 'considerations' take a very different form today. It is hard to imagine cream cheeses surreptitiously changing hands within the corridors of power!

The first point to note is that David found himself with an opportunity to be of great service to Israel because he had been obedient (to his father) when given a simple errand to run. Making the most of opportunities given to us is usually more fruitful than thrashing about looking for opportunities that may not exist. David also discovered that obedience and faithfulness in one task had led him to the opportunity to do greater things for God. Jesus said something similar in the parable of the ten servants.[4]

The second point is that David had assessed his own worth. He reviewed his ability to overcome the lion and the bear in the interests of saving the flock from destruction. He sensed that he could apply his past experience to a current situation. We, too, come to learn that everything we have hitherto experienced in life is a preparation for the present and the future. All life experience, good and bad, painful and joyful, has relevance.

Consider James, a man in his forties who was about to be ordained and was visiting several parishes with a view to being licensed as an assistant curate. An interview with a parish priest seemed to be going rather well. They discussed all that would be required of the new curate and what support there would be available to him after his ordination. Just as an agreement was about to be reached, the parish priest picked up James' application forms and studied them one more time. Then he looked at James and said: 'You do realise that you must leave behind you all your previous work experience. It is of no relevance in parochial ministry.' The priest had forgotten the story of David. James went away saddened and sought another post. He was successful and went on to a much-valued ministry.

James had understood that everything in his life to the present moment had been God-given. He was the youngest of seven children and his father had walked out on his mother when James was 9 years old. James' work experience started when he was old enough to carry in the coal for the fire and to wash up the dishes after eight people had eaten. His work experience since leaving school had included working in the cellar of a hotel; working with other sales staff in a busy department store and being stationed on the customer service counter in the periods immediately before and after Christmas. He had risen to supervisor and finally to store manager. In his spare time he had run a youth club and helped with parties for people with learning difficulties. The words of the parish priest rang in his ears: 'You do realise that you must leave behind you all your previous work experience. It is of no relevance in parochial ministry.'

David brought to the battlefield all his previous life experiences. He brought something else too. David had been secretly anointed by Samuel. Samuel took the horn of oil and anointed him in the presence of his brothers, and the Spirit of the Lord came upon David. The Lord was with him from that day onwards.[5]

James, by his baptism, was anointed by the Spirit of God. The Lord was with him from that day onwards. The Lord had known him since before he was formed in his mother's womb.[6] He had known him and called him by his name. His hand was guiding him. James was called into the service of others long before he was ordained as a deacon, a servant. James could see that the Lord had led him to this point and had equipped him for the next phase of his ministry. He would have lots to learn about parochial ministry but he would come to it with what he had: his life experience, his work experience, his experience of people – angry people; frustrated people; people needing guidance and leadership; vulnerable and fragile people. He had, too, his theological reflection, partly based on a review of his life so far. He had also his ministerial training. James, like David, was poised to do great things for God. James, like David, had been faithful with what he had been given to do so far, and he was pleasing to God. Like David, James had sometimes been an 'impudent young rascal'[7] and God had used that, too.

Here we have a number of clues as to how to have a strategic approach to our calling, especially when our resources are limited by weariness. David used the opportunities given to him and he knew his own worth. He was able to make a truthful assessment of himself. He made himself available to the service of his king, confident in the God who had anointed him with his Spirit. He was able to make connections between past successes (and mistakes) and the current challenge. Yesterday's lion becomes today's Goliath!

We return to our story after Saul had given David permission to go out and fight the Philistine. Saul gave David his own tunic to wear and put on his head a helmet of bronze and a coat of mail to wear. He then fastened his sword over David's tunic. David was not at all keen to wear all that heavy armour. He had not been used to it and so he took it off. He rejected the cumbersome armour and weapons that others favoured and chose instead to use his sling and five smooth stones. With these he set out to meet the Philistine.

Another dimension of a strategic approach to our calling is the ability to evaluate the resources available to us. So many people want to weigh us down with advice and to insist that we do things their way. We need to find the courage to say, 'No thank you. It was kind of you to offer me your bronze helmet but I need to be bare-headed for this one.' We have all been glad to receive advice and all been glad to borrow the experience of others. If we are not to be bowed down by the 'armour' of others but free to move with ease in the service of the Lord, we must be discerning and not be afraid to pick and choose from among the options around us. Teaching ourselves to reject offers of advice or help as well as teaching ourselves to accept them may, in itself, be a major challenge.

Few people will know all that we have been and all that we have done in our lives. Few will know the extent of our capabilities and few (thankfully) will know our capacity for making a mess of things. Whatever those capabilities, and whatever that mess, it is *our* mess and *our* ability. God has blessed both and uses both, and does marvellous things with them.

My concern is not for those who have succeeded in achieving a sensible balance in these things and from a position of health and strength. I am concerned for the weary: for those who have been wearied by past battles fought (won or lost) or who have been wearing the wrong armour. There are those who are wearied by waving their heavy sword in the air, hoping it finds its mark, instead of learning to parry and to thrust effectively.

Consider Father Jonathan, a devoted parish priest with many years' experience of parish ministry in Canada. Every evening at six o'clock, Father Jonathan would meet with his curates to pray. They would take it in turns to lead the Divine Office, the Prayer of the Church. Jonathan would arrive in church a few minutes before six and slump heavily into a pew in the little side chapel. He would lean his arms on the pew in front, and bury his head under his arm. He would appear wretched and exhausted. His colleagues feared for his health.

One of the curates would lead the service. The versicles, read enthusiastically by the officiant, would meet with differing responses from the tiny congregation. The other ministers' responses were clear but those of Father Jonathan were mumbled from under his armpit. They were delivered with a sigh so deep that Sheol could be glimpsed!

The question running through the minds of the curates was this: 'What dreadful weight or burden was Father Jonathan carrying? What had he been doing today that had exhausted him so?' Part of the answer would emerge at their regular team meeting. They would discuss who had been visited and what particular pastoral concerns there were. All was said and done without disclosing anything too personal and without breaking the seal of the confessional.

Jonathan disclosed how he had tried to visit a woman in the parish (several miles away from the house) and how he had visited her home three times that week only to find that she was not in. One of the curates had the temerity to suggest that Father Jonathan might telephone the woman first and arrange a mutually convenient time to call. The parish priest drew himself up to his full height and, looking over his half-spectacles, said: 'I hate the telephone. It is so impersonal.'

Over the following months, the newest and most junior curate, newly ordained, a product of a different generation of clergy, observed how often his parish priest seemed to make abortive attempts to visit. He noticed how often Father Jonathan would use the most long-winded and complicated ways of doing anything. The curate knew that he lacked real experience and that, one day, he might see things differently, but for now he could only see a good priest becoming exhausted to very little good effect. He tried to emulate his apparent capacity for work (having no other earthly role model) until the poor young thing became ill from exhaustion and of little use to anyone. He fell into the trap of believing that weariness is next to godliness (and even holiness). Once the young priest recognised that it is not, he stopped trying to follow his senior colleague's example, and his ministry became much more fruitful and fulfilling.

David chose five smooth pebbles. He did not put all his trust and faith into one small stone. He had other options. Each of us may recall times when we have gone off in the wrong direction: made a mistake. We may simply not have understood what God wanted of us, but we may look back and see how he redeemed the mistake. We might see not only what we learned but what God did with and through us, even when we were in error.

When we undertake something new for the Lord, or when we set ourselves a new and modest target for our recovery from the cause of our weariness, it is as well to consider all the options. David had more than one option. We take into account all the factors known to us. We take our time to select the appropriate, small smooth stone. We need to think things through. By aiming carefully and using the weapon with which he was most familiar, David brought down the Philistine.

The triumph of David, in the face of overwhelming odds, is the victory of right, truth and sincerity. The stone to the forehead of Goliath becomes a symbol of the need to be strategic, to manage ourselves, our resources, and to focus our energies. As best we can, we make every pebble count because we have used precious resources in the casting of it.

Books have been written, seminars given, and training events run, to teach us how to do these things. They are all worth exploring and adapting to our own needs and circumstances. Some aspects of ordering our resources are instinctive and others need to be learned. They are all aspects of 'management' that some find so irritating. Under the guidance of his

Spirit at work in us and through us, our mentors and others, every word, deed and action, every bit of our human and personal resources can be employed appropriately and effectively to the glory of God. I think we call this stewardship.

References
1. 1 Samuel 16:12b
2. John 10:14
3. 1 Samuel 17:15, 20
4. Luke 19:17
5. 1 Samuel 16:13
6. Jeremiah 1:5
7. 1 Samuel 17:28b

Focus for reflection

Like good stewards of the manifold grace of God,
serve one another with whatever gift each of you has received.
(1 Peter 4:10)

Suggestions for prayer

Lord, you have given us so much 'know-how'
    and have given us examples in Scripture
    of how you have been strategic
    in the creation and the salvation of the world.
Thank you for numerous examples
    of how your servants have managed well
    the personal and material resources you have provided.
Help us to be good stewards of your grace;
    and of your generous provision. Amen.

In my weariness, Lord,
    I have little energy to spare
    and none to waste on activities contrary to your will.
I know that your grace is sufficient for me
    and that you call me to use it wisely.
Grant me your wisdom and the gift of discernment
    so that I may, more often, focus my energy
    on life-enhancing and kingdom-building activity. Amen.

I know you to be a gracious God
  who is waiting to be gracious to me:
  to grant me my heart's desire.
Help me to see that desire and choice
  can come from you too.
Help me to sense where you are drawing me
  and to avoid being driven by other forces. Amen.

Questions for those alone

Can you think of ways to save energy and to be more effective?

Is all your activity 'demand led' or do you have some freedom of choice?

After careful thought, dare to bring your deepest desires to God.

Suggestions for group discussion

Can the Church learn anything from modern-day management theory or is God at work only in the Church and nowhere else?

Do we make unrealistic demands upon each other's time and resources?

Is all our activity focused on building the Kingdom of God or do we sometimes make the Kingdom the excuse for doing what we want to do?

Does God ever motivate us to do what *he* wants us to do through doing what *we* want to do?

Chapter 7

' 'Tis good, Lord, to be here':
God at work in sleep, in glory,
and in shadow

There are many incidents in the Gospels that might encourage
the weary. In this chapter, I have focused on two of them. They
are intimate occasions witnessed by only a handful of people.

The first is the account of Jesus and his disciples in the Garden
of Gethsemane.[1] On that occasion Jesus had taken Peter,
James and John away from the others (remember that Judas
Iscariot had already gone). Leaving the three, Jesus went a little
apart from them and poured out his heart to his Father in the
most heart-rending words. To understand what happened in the
Garden of Gethsemane it may be helpful to reflect on the events
that led up to it.

Jesus had entered Jerusalem to cries of: 'Hosanna to the Son
of David!'[2] People laid down their coats, cut down palm
branches, and strewed them in his way. The disciples must
have been thrilled to hear these words of adulation and what
they might have considered to be the beginnings of the recognition of Jesus as Lord, as Messiah, as Son of God. The days
that followed were packed with activity. There were the challenges to the authority of Jesus and the attempts to entrap him.
There was the incident in which Jesus over-turned the tables
of the moneychangers in the Temple. The crowds were torn
in their opinions and loyalties. There was agitation and in-
credulity everywhere. The disciples had seen so much in the
past three years but nothing like the sights, sounds, and atmosphere of Jerusalem in those few days.

Finally there was that poignant supper in the upper room.
There were the words of Jesus, especially his passionate dis-
course on love and the deeply moving and mysterious words
that accompanied the taking, blessing, breaking and sharing of

bread and wine. There was the humbling experience of the Master washing their feet.[3] They had eaten, it was late and they were exhausted. They were anxious and mystified. They dared not own what they knew. They were concerned for Jesus who was so obviously distraught and heart-sore, yet they probably felt helpless and did not know what to say or do. Sleep would be a natural response, a welcome relief, and a very human way of coping with it all.

When we compare the Gospel accounts of the incidents in the Garden of Gethsemane we may be struck by the differences between them. John does not record the sleeping disciples at all, but that should not surprise us since scholars tell us that John chose what he recorded to support the theological points he was making. Matthew, Mark, and Luke all record Jesus as instructing the three disciples to sit, to stay awake or to pray. He calls them to be active but they are overcome by sleep. Given the recent events, they had plenty of reasons to sleep.

Matthew, Mark, and Luke all record that Jesus returned to the three disciples and, finding them asleep, questioned their inability to keep awake and watch. Dear and compassionate Luke records that Jesus found them asleep 'worn out by grief'.[4] Only Matthew and Mark include the stinging and seemingly contemptuous remark: 'The spirit is willing but the flesh is weak.' Luke is the only one to record that an angel ministered to Jesus, and he is the only to spare Peter, James and John from the humiliation of the retort. Given that only two of the four Gospel writers record the remark, it amazes me how easily it trips off the tongue of Christians. Often it is used as a rebuke for not doing all that we are willing to do. What makes it more cutting, and what makes it such a vicious weapon in the mouth of the self-righteous, is that little word 'but'. The spirit is willing 'but' the flesh is weak. What a horrid word 'but' can be when used in this way. It is like a hand raised in our face and often prefaces bad news: 'This is a lovely picture, Matilda, *but* shouldn't Mummy have *two* legs?'

We might say, when we are being given feed-back or an opinion: 'I feel a "but" coming.' Much of the time this may not bother us. It is perhaps when we are weary or dispirited, or when we are exhausted by grief, and therefore vulnerable, that a critical 'but' can finish us off. If it came from the mouth of Jesus, I believe that it would be full of love and compassion. I cannot believe that Jesus intended his remark to be devastating and guilt-inducing. At best it is a statement of fact. If Jesus did not intend to injure (and my hunch is that Luke did not think so either) then we should not be in a hurry to quote this remark pejoratively.

Dare we say that Jesus was close to doing what other humans may do? He was under pressure. He was stressed. We hold the belief that Jesus was fully human: like us in every way except sin. The metaphor of sweat pouring from him like great drops of blood suggests stress by anyone's definition. Jesus returned to his disciples and found them sleeping. If it had not been the sinless Lord, but one of us who found them so, might we not have been tempted to rebuke them, even though they were not at fault? Sometimes we call it the 'kick the dog' syndrome: the unjust transference of anxiety to another and usually to an innocent victim. This is inconsistent with a belief in a sinless Jesus. Did Jesus really rebuke his disciples on this occasion or was it a remark based in love, compassion and understanding? Was it not something which stated the situation perfectly but not pejoratively? To the wearied and the bruised, the difference may be crucial to how they understand God's view of their current state.

'The spirit is willing but the flesh is weak.' There are ways of saying this that are compassionate, spoken out of a shared understanding of the way things are. Yes, our spirit is willing to follow Jesus all the way. Yes, our flesh is weak. We know that so well. If we do use the expression, we may adapt it so that our meaning is clear. Simply, and as an observation of reality in our life, we might say: 'The spirit is willing; the flesh weak.'

Meanwhile, back in the Garden of Gethsemane, eight other disciples were allowed to sleep in peace. No rebuke. No condemnation. Perhaps the way that Peter, James and John were singled out for special duty tells us something, according to Matthew and Mark anyway, about the commitment expected from those in leadership, but we should remember that the other eight disciples went on to do great things for God too, presumably unaware of the instructions and the remark to the chosen three.

This time of sleeping would be followed by a time when the skies would darken at the death of Jesus. Then the disciples would experience the glory of the resurrection and finally, Jesus would be taken from them in a cloud. The disciples had already experienced a little of this process: sleep, glory, cloud. The occasion was the Transfiguration of Jesus.

We come, then, to the account of how Jesus took Peter, James and John up a mountainside, and going slightly apart, as he so often did, he left them whilst he prayed. Inevitably, they fell asleep.

Jesus knew what was ahead of him and his disciples. He knew too that his disciples were weary; they were becoming dispirited due to the overwhelming demands being made upon Jesus for his counsel, his teaching, and his healing. The disciples had shared the rigours of the ministry of Jesus. They had slept under the stars and had roamed from town to town, village to village. At first it was an adventure, now they might be wondering how things would turn out. They had been away from their homes and families for nearly three years. They had left them to follow Jesus. Most of them, most of the time, did not regret that, but, in the wee small hours, when the wind blew chill and the Lord was lost in prayer and contemplation, they might have longed for the comfort of their own bed by their own fire, surrounded by those they loved.

Jesus knew they needed encouragement: to be 'encouraged', to be made courageous, for there was worse to come. It would be particularly demanding for those who would hold positions of leadership in the Church, but that was in the future. For now they huddled together on a hillside whilst Jesus went apart to pray. A colleague of mine likens himself to the sheepdog of the shepherd. I regard him as an associate shepherd, sharing with me in the ministry of the Good

Shepherd; but, in this instance, the image of a faithful pet dog springs to mind. It follows on one's heels. The minute one sits down, it lies at one's feet and immediately goes to sleep.

There are many kinds of sleep and we can only guess what kind of sleep the disciples experienced on this occasion. It may have been the heavy sleep of exhaustion: a sleep which does not necessarily refresh us. It is a sleep from which we wake reluctantly. We may be aware of our surroundings but still be unable to move.

Perhaps the disciples needed to shut out the reality of their life. The fantasies and realms of near-sleep and slumber may have been infinitely preferable to anxiety, homesickness, despair or grief. In exploring possible types and causes of sleep, I hope the reader will not come too quickly to an opinion that the disciples' sleep was the result of boredom, disloyalty or lack of interest. Our reflection on the Garden of Gethsemane may have already taught us the dangers of such prejudgement.

For whatever reason, the chosen three were asleep. They were unaware that Jesus was surrounded by light. They too were bathed in reflected light, but they did not know it. When our daughter was very young, she would close her eyes and, because she could not see, she would presume that she could not be seen. We too, might be tempted to presume that because we do not see light, there is no light. In an earlier chapter we considered the 'night' experience and recovered its value. The disciples asleep on the mountain whilst Jesus was in communion with Moses and Elijah reminds us that God is at work even as we sleep. We are bathed in light that warms our soul. It transfigures us and heals us whilst we remain unconscious of it. Some people can recall the day, the hour, and the moment when they knew they were healed, restored or forgiven. Others can look back, comparing themselves now with the way they once were, and can attest to the transfiguring and healing grace of God, but they are not conscious of how or when that happened. A poster on that mountainside (or at our bedside) might read: 'Humanity unconscious, God at work.'

Jesus lives to make intercession for us to the Father.[5] When we rest, Jesus prays. When rest is all that is available to us, we finally let the Spirit of God pray in us. It is a pity that it takes the removal of all our consciousness, power, and control, before we can let God take over.

It is the same with others who want to help. We might resist their help because we are reluctant to be out of control. Independence, which we admire, becomes stubbornness (in ourselves and others) which we cannot admire. Finally we give in and let others watch and pray. How we feel the benefit! Our first obedience might be to rest, to sleep and to let the healing and growing process continue unhindered.

Something stirred Peter, James and John. Perhaps it was the brilliance of Tabor's light. The light called them to consciousness. It may have been a call that lasted a few seconds, or it may have been much longer. This awakening can teach us so much. It is our own experience of becoming conscious of God's activity in our life. It is an awakening to the irradiating light of Christ penetrating the cells and fibres of our being. We sense the call of God like young Samuel in the Temple: 'Samuel! Samuel!' the Lord calls. With some help from Eli, Samuel responds: 'Speak, Lord, your servant is listening.'[6]

Somewhere between wakefulness and sleep; somewhere between sleep and awakening, we are open and vulnerable. It is the state that hypnotists use to influence the subconscious mind. It was the state that young Samuel was in. We might make (quite literally) a conscious effort to hear God's call. We might work at it, making regular appointments with God to pray or to read the Scriptures, hoping and expecting that we might find the answer to our question: 'Lord, are you calling me to this or to that?' We find it does not come (at least it does not come that way). A personal tragedy, redundancy, bereavement or perhaps a life-threatening illness leaves us vulnerable and undefended. The call comes gently at first. It becomes insistent. We wake slowly to Tabor's light and, without thinking, we sigh: 'Here I am, Lord. Your servant is listening.' God will not be allocated an appointment: the Spirit blows where it will.[7] The call comes through openness and vulnerability.

The sleepy-headed three woke to the brilliant vision of Jesus in conversation with Moses and Elijah. 'Wow!' we might say. Peter said: 'It is good, Lord, that we are here. Let us put up three tents, one for you, one for Moses and one for Elijah.' The disciples just wanted to keep them there, to go on enjoying the vision. And what did it mean? Moses, the authority figure for the ancient law of God; Elijah, giant among the prophets; and Jesus, the carpenter's son from Nazareth, whom they had begun to know as the Son of God. Whatever it meant, glory found them. Words by Carey Landry say it so well:

We behold the splendour of God,
shining on the face of Jesus.
. . . his beauty transforms us,
the wonder of Presence abiding.
Transparent hearts give reflection of Tabor's light within . . .
Jesus, Lord of Glory, . . .
how good to be with you; how good to share your light.[8]

Jesus knew the chosen three needed a glimpse of glory, a sign that all that they were suffering was not in vain: that it did all mean something. It was like an unexpected shaft of sunlight between the clouds on a cold February day which brings a little warmth to the bones. Perhaps they thought they were dreaming. They knew the Scriptures and were familiar with a God who speaks through dreams. Perhaps they blinked twice, and pinched themselves. Having had respite for their bodies, the disciples are given refreshment for their spirit. They needed just a glimpse of glory, and Jesus gave it them as a gift.

Phase two then, of the Transfiguration, is the glimpse of the glory yet to come. It would encourage the followers of Jesus and it would strengthen them as they came down the mountain and set their faces towards Jerusalem and the horrors to come. They would need every blessing to cope with the passion and death of Jesus and to survive; better than that, to celebrate the glorious rising of Christ from the dead, to fill the air with alleluias!

We too are given glimpses of glory. They may come upon us unexpectedly. We cannot contrive them or even expect them. They are a gift but we may be able to dispose ourselves to receiving such gifts by trying to keep ourselves open to the possibility of them. So often we focus our attention on the resolution of our great problems. We seek the cure, the settlement, the final outcome but we miss the signs of glory: the glimpses of the God who is near and cares deeply about us. We may be looking so hard towards the door, waiting for him to appear, that we miss the glimpse of the hem of his garment as it blows gently in the breeze, almost out of sight.

To go round looking for glory, or to exhort others to do the same, can be counter-productive. We may cheerfully encourage people to make the best of a situation but I am suspicious of people who do so with a permanent and benign grin on their face, especially if I am feeling angry or frustrated. There are, however, opportunities to help people to recognise a glimpse of glory amid the devastation of their life. I have been blessed in this way by others, and have been grateful for their sensitive ministry.

Looking for God's gift of a glimpse of glory is not the same as seeking pleasure. 'If it makes you happy, do it,' is something we hear all too often. Hedonism is the enemy of spiritual growth because it seduces us into idolatry. We make 'other gods' of self-satisfiers. They are, in the long run, no satisfier at all. Hedonism encourages us to be self-absorbed. Looking for signs and glimpses of glory requires us to turn our faces to the Son. We are not sunbathers, worshipping the great god 'all-over tan'. We are 'Son-bathers': bathed, even briefly and unexpectedly, in Tabor's light. We Son-bathe in dappled light!

In the third phase of the Transfiguration story, the focus of attention is drawn from the glorious light to a bright cloud that overshadowed the disciples. It was then that they heard the voice of God: not in the sleep or in the glory, but in the shadow.

We have considered the role and value of sleep. We have recognised it as a time of growth, refreshment and renewal. In this chapter we have considered sleep as respite from grief and anxiety. We have reflected on God's gift in glimpses of glory, recognising how they are surprise presents, but presents we might easily miss if we are not disposed to receive them. Times of passivity, rest, and sleep are punctuated by times of activity, 'tent building' and of glory. In between, there are times of shadow and of cloud. The cloud may be dense and black as we experience grief and loss; doubt and despair. There are too, the times of 'bright' cloud, like that experienced by Peter, James and John on the mountain of the Transfiguration.

I believe that a Christian experiences all these moods and phases, but that the experience of bright cloud predominates. We cannot live on the mountain top. We have to return to a world which can feel alien to our spirit: a place where we do battle with evil. It is also the place to 'soak up' the anger, the bitterness, the cynicism and the derision of non-believers and believers alike. All this is off-set by our experiences of love, joy, peace, patience, kindness, goodness, gentleness, faithfulness and self-control.[9] We see courage and heroism all around us. Our experience of 'cloud' is a common one but it is often 'bright cloud' and it fills us with hope and confidence that 'all things work together well for those who love God'.[10]

First, the weary disciples were asleep when the glory came, reminding us that just because we are not attending or not fit enough to stay awake and watch, it does not mean there is no glory, no vision. God shines his light upon us whether we are aware of it or not. Sometimes it is only when we are too weary to sin or too broken down to resist him that he can bathe us in his light: like dozing briefly in the sun and absorbing the vitamin D!

Secondly, the disciples did see the vision. They looked at Jesus and interacted with him. They tried to hold on to the vision and to understand its significance for them. It was a brief respite to be enjoyed. It was a bonus, a moment of glory, a gift, a joy. It fed them, it nourished them and it strengthened them for what lay ahead. It was over so soon: the vision gone. Later they would recall it, tell the story, write it down. They would go through the horrors of the following weeks and would survive:

and better than survive! They would come down from the mountain to the real world in which the forces of darkness are pitted against the forces of light, and with God's help they would overcome them.

Thirdly, they heard the voice of God, not when they were asleep and not when they beheld the glory, but in the cloud, in the gloom, in the half-light that teases and tantalises and distorts. It was not in sleep that God spoke (like he did to Samuel). It was not in the glorious light that God spoke; rather, Peter did all the talking! God spoke in the bright cloud that overshadowed the disciples. God speaks to us in the dark, the doubt, the pessimism and the confusion.

In other parts of Scripture we understand an 'overshadowing' as a blessing from God and as an occasion when he will do something wonderful in us. The annunciation of the Lord to the Blessed Virgin Mary is a wonderful example of 'overshadowing'.[11]

To appreciate light we need shadow and darkness. If we walk into a room and see an illuminated Christmas tree, we might, at first, think of it as 'all lit up'. On closer inspection we see that the illumination is made up of a number of tiny lights. Behind the lights and between the branches there are deep and dark caverns, which give definition and depth to the decoration. The lights seem to occur at random but in reality they are in measured distances from each other and have been carefully arranged to create the best effect. They are a series of little lights that light a pilgrim's path. They link the present with the past and the future.

Consider the lace-maker's art. The intricate pattern made by the complex interplay of bobbins produces exquisite and breath-taking fabric, but the effect is fully appreciated only when the lace is held against a dark background. It is the holes that make the lace come to life!

My point is that, for Christians, 'bright cloud' is the typical state. The weary Christian should take heart and not be alarmed. It is the state in which we are most likely to hear God's voice. We 'hear' it through prayer, through reading the Scriptures and other writings. We 'hear' it in liturgy, worship, preaching and teaching. We 'hear' it in the words and experiences of those around us. We 'hear' it in exclamations of joy and laughter. We 'hear' it in sighs of sorrow and we 'hear' it in silence. It is an experience of bright cloud that overshadows us. What we hear is this: 'This is my Son, my Beloved, on whom my favour rests.' We 'hear' our Father speak of his Son and we know that, as his sometimes weary children, he means us too.

References
1. Matthew 26:36-44; Mark 14:32-41a; Luke 22:39-46
2. Matthew 21:1-12
3. John 13:1-15
4. Luke 22:45, REV
5. Hebrews 7:25
6. 1 Samuel 3
7. cf John 3:8
8. © Copyright 1976, North American Liturgy Resources (NALR), 5536 NE Hassalo, Portland, Oregon 97213, USA. All rights reserved. Used by permission.
9. Galatians 5: 22-24
10. Romans 8:28
11. Luke 1:26-38, especially verse 35a

Focus for reflection

Speak Lord, your servant is listening.
(1 Samuel 3:10b)

Suggestions for prayer

Lord, I am looking for meaning and purpose
    in my weariness.
I look at the cross
    and see exhaustion that saved the world
    and hear 'It is accomplished'.
I often feel that I am wearied for no great purpose.
Help me to believe
    that my weariness has value in your sight.
Help me to hold on: to trust you.
Sometimes I find it very difficult. Amen.

Thank you, Lord,
    for the times you have gladdened my heart
    with glimpses of glory.
I see them in nature, in human relationships.
On dark days, help me to revisit, in my mind,
    the places that were filled with light.
Help me to hold on
    to the moments when I have cried:
    'It is good, Lord, to be here.' Amen.

Lord, you have shown me
    how I can manage with limited light.
Help me to own your presence in 'bright cloud':
    to sense the aura of your presence
    and the corona of your abiding. Amen.

Questions for those alone

Can you recall 'glimpses of glory', 'mountaintop experiences'? If you can, savour them now. Rehearse how you will revisit them in your mind when dark clouds gather or when you cannot sleep.

Perhaps you are experiencing the dark cloud of not knowing, not understanding: overshadowed by misfortune. Can you adjust your eyes to the half-light, and live in cloud for a little longer? Can you hold on to the One who says of you: 'This is my beloved'?

Does it help to know that, although you are not conscious of it, the Lord is bathing you in healing light?

Suggestions for group discussion

Can Christians become addicted to 'mountaintop' experiences? If so, how harmful is their addiction, to them and to those around them?

Have we ever diminished or dismissed people's sense of hopelessness, or infuriated them by being overly cheerful or supercilious? Is there a better way to help?

How do we help each other to adjust to changing 'light'?